D0012083

Time, Rocks, and the Rockies

A Geologic Guide
to Roads and Trails
of Rocky Mountain National Park

Halka Chronic

Scott W. Starratt
Dept. of Paleontology
U. C. Berkeley
Berkeley, Ca. 94720

MOUNTAIN PRESS PUBLISHING COMPANY
MISSOULA, 1984

All rights reserved. No part of this book may be reproduced or transmitted in any form or by any means, electronic or mechanical, including photocopying, recording, or by any information storage and retrieval system, without permission in writing from the Publisher.

Copyright © 1984
Mountain Press Publishing Co.

Library of Congress Cataloging in Publication Data

Chronic, Halka.
   Time, rocks, and the Rockies.

   1. Geology—Colorado—Rocky Mountain National Park—
Guide-books. 2. Rocky Mountain National Park (Colo.)—
Description and travel—Guide-books. I. Title.
QE92.R6C48   1984   917.88'30433   84-8429
ISBN 0-87842-172-6

Scott W. Starratt
Dept. of Paleontology
U. C. Berkeley
Berkeley, Ca. 94720

Contents

I Of Rocks and Time

The Concept of Time 1
A Few Geologic Basics...7
Geologic Architecture..12
Weathering and Erosion...17
The Growth of the Rockies 18

II Roadside Geology: Getting to the Park

U.S. 36 Lyons to Rocky Mountain National Park 25
U.S. 34 Loveland to Rocky Mountain National Park...........30
U.S. 34 Granby to Rocky Mountain National Park 38
Colorado 7 Lyons to Estes Park.....................................41

III Roadside Geology: Park Roads

Trail Ridge Road — a Two-way Guide 47
Moraine Park—Bear Lake Road...70
Old Fall River Road 75

IV Trailside Geology

Bear Lake—Dream Lake—Emerald Lake Trail...................83
Glacier Gorge Trail 87
Loch Vale—Sky Pond Trail...92
Fern Lake—Odessa Lake Trail..93
Easts Longs Peak Trail 97
Chasm Lake Trail 105
Lawn Lake Trail..107
Colorado River—Little Yellowstone Trail 110

Glossary 115
Selected References 119

At 14,255 feet the highest summit in Rocky Mountain National Park, Longs Peak rises above Mills Lake and Glacier Gorge.

Preface

Here it is on the backbone of the continent — Rocky Mountain National Park, a place of handsome peaks and glacier-gouged canyons, of forests, meadows, lakes, and streams, of snowfields and tundra, high country representative of the Rocky Mountains as a whole and yet unique in its own exciting beauty.

Here in a few miles we travel from summer to winter, from the shimmering July of the Great Plains to the chill of the arctic north, ranging thousands of horizontal miles in just a few thousand vertical feet.

Here, too, we can move back in time, from the present into the past, to reconstruct the story told in the rocks — a story painted boldly on cliffs and in yawning precipices, detailed in lakes and ravines and hills of rocky rubble, murmured by the wind whistling among the crags. A story reaching back thousands, millions, even billions of years.

Well named, the Rocky Mountains do not conceal their secrets from us beneath mantles of soil, nor are those secrets hidden with blacktop and concrete. Here we can see ancient rocks twisted and distorted, time and again lifted as towering mountains, time and again worn down, time and again buried beneath crushing burdens of younger rock. Here, too, we find evidence of moving rivers of ice — glaciers — that not too long ago helped to shape the landforms of the Rockies, even as larger glaciers shaped the northern part of the continent. And we can observe even now the unending attack of water and wind, of frost and ice, of the ever-present downward pull of gravity.

This book is designed for those with little or no geologic training. I hope students and professional geologists will find it useful, too, or at least enjoyable. For geology is a joyful science, calling its practitioners out of doors, into the sun and wind (and sometimes the rain and snow and hail) to learn about our island planet and what makes it tick. In Rocky Mountain Park getting out of doors takes us from the hurly-burly and polluted air of cities and highways to the clean, clear freshness of the mountains, to quiet trails and moments of solitude, wherein we may ponder the great questions posed by the earth itself.

As you follow the roads described here, I hope you will stop and step out of your car at frequent intervals to look more closely at the scenes about you. To see the distant landscape, use binoculars if you have them. Examine the closer rocks, noting their texture and color and mineral makeup. Heft loose rocks in your hand; feel their surfaces, rough or smooth. Those who walk the trails will huff and puff enough to welcome frequent stops; deliberately I have logged the trails in the upward direction! Each road described here deserves half a day; you may want more for Trail Ridge Road. Most of the trails can be walked in a few hours, if you are in good shape, but a full day allows time for leisurely geologic browsing along the way. Remember that high-altitude air is thin, and don't overtax yourself.

The East Longs Peak trail needs a full day and then some — start before dawn and carry a flashlight. Many hikers on this trail will not want to go beyond Chasm Lake or the Keyhole. For both roads and trails you'll want a warm jacket and perhaps a cap. The Park Service recommends that you carry your own drinking water.

Because of their small scale, the maps in this book do not identify all the lakes, canyons, and peaks mentioned in this book. I strongly recommend the use of a good topographic map in conjunction with the book, particularly for those who intend to hike on the trails. A topographic map of Rocky Mountain Park published by Trails Illustrated is available at Park visitor centers; it is printed on waterproof, tearproof paper — a big advantage for hikers — and contains up-to-date road and trail information. Hikers and climbers who go beyond the ends of established trails will of course want more detailed U.S. Geological Survey quadrangle maps, also available at visitor centers.

The geologic map in Chapter II is derived from the map of Colorado published by the USGS in 1979, with changes suggested by USGS and other geologists. It is necessarily generalized, but defines in a broad way the rocks found in various parts of the park. Geologic mapping in the park is an ongoing project of students and faculty at nearby universities, and there will no doubt be many changes in maps of the park in years to come.

In gathering together the information for this book I have drawn from published literature by U.S. Geological Survey and other scientists, and from unpublished theses by University of Colorado, Colorado State University, and Colorado School of Mines graduate students, backed up by my own observations. I have driven each road and hiked each trail, the better to give you a blow-by-blow account of geologic features along them. Photographs are mine unless otherwise indicated.

I wish to thank all those who have made my task enjoyable — from National Park Service rangers and naturalists to visitors who expressed their interest in the story told by the rocks. I particularly thank those who waded through the manuscript of this book and gave freely of comments and suggestions: Park Naturalist Glen Kaye and geologists Dave Alt, Felicie and Mike Williams, and John Chronic. Many others offered suggestions on specific points, and I thank them as well, along with the geologists and naturalists of past and present on whose work I necessarily leaned. I express my appreciation also to the National Park Service and the Rocky Mountain Nature Association, Inc., for their backing during the field work and preparation of this book.

With its twisted, gnarled banding, resembling ancient wood, this schist is easily recognized.

I.
Of Rocks and Time

The Concept of Time

If the earth is 46 years old, human beings have lived upon it for about eleven days. During the last twelve minutes or so these unusually inquisitive creatures have tried to keep track of their own history. In the last two minutes they have made some strong attempts to decipher the long, long story of the planet they live on. Yet only within the last eight seconds have they developed a systematic understanding of its origins and the changes that have taken place upon and within it.

Geologic time measures in such overwhelmingly large quantities that I have scaled it down into easily associated, everyday terms to bring its immensity within understandable bounds. Now let's see what the Earth's time scale really is: The planet is now thought to be about 4.6 billion years old. Man — *Homo* — has walked two-footed on its surface for something like 3 million years. About 2450 years ago Herodotus made history by chronicling the political and military struggles between Persia and Greece. Geology as a science was born a little over 400 years ago when Georgius Agricola published detailed observations of mineral deposits of Bohemia (now western Czechoslovakia) and reasoned deductions about the rocks in which they occurred. And the plate tectonics theory that elegantly interprets the origins and migrations of the present continents was born less than 25 years ago.

Against the Earth's gigantic time frame, geologists have placed the **geologic time scale** — a calendar of sorts, with named intervals that are useful in comparing rocks of different

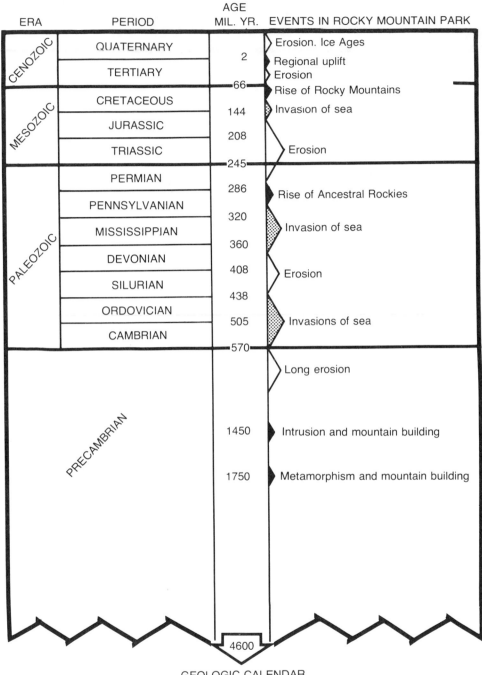

ERA	PERIOD	AGE MIL. YR.	EVENTS IN ROCKY MOUNTAIN PARK
CENOZOIC	QUATERNARY	2	Erosion. Ice Ages
			Regional uplift
	TERTIARY		Erosion
		66	Rise of Rocky Mountains
MESOZOIC	CRETACEOUS	144	Invasion of sea
	JURASSIC	208	
	TRIASSIC	245	Erosion
PALEOZOIC	PERMIAN	286	Rise of Ancestral Rockies
	PENNSYLVANIAN	320	
	MISSISSIPPIAN	360	Invasion of sea
	DEVONIAN	408	Erosion
	SILURIAN	438	
	ORDOVICIAN	505	Invasions of sea
	CAMBRIAN	570	
PRECAMBRIAN			Long erosion
		1450	Intrusion and mountain building
		1750	Metamorphism and mountain building
		4600	

GEOLOGIC CALENDAR

ages. The calendar developed at a time when there was no known way to pin down, for sure, the ages of rock units — no way to tell whether they were 4000 or 40,000 or 40,000,000 years old. But by studying and mapping recognizable rock units, called **formations**, and their fossils, geologists were able to figure out which rocks were older and which younger. Eventually the calendar became detailed enough for comparing rocks of different areas and even different continents.

Nowadays radioactive elements, which decay into "daughter" products at very precise rates, give us much more accurate ways of determining the numerical ages of rocks. The old geologic calendar, though, is so well embedded in geologic thought and literature that geologists are not about to give it up, so it is presented here, along with the newest numerical data (in millions of years before the present) for the long-standing major divisions of the old calendar.

Before all those names turn you away, let me say that not many of the calendar divisions pertain to the history of the particular patch of earth known as Rocky Mountain National Park. You should notice, though, that the geologic calendar divides geologic time into **eras** and **periods** — the "months" and "weeks" of geologic time. (For detailed studies, periods are also divided into **epochs**, not used in this book.) Unlike months and weeks, all eras or all periods are not of nearly the same length, nor are there the same number of periods in every era. This is because the scale was pieced together from known rocks, mostly in Europe, that represented different lengths of time, with gaps also of different lengths between them, and because the farther back we go in geologic time, the scarcer is the rock record, much of it having been worn away by erosion or covered up with younger rocks. We know lots more about the most recent or **Cenozoic Era** than we do about the **Paleozoic** or **Precambrian Eras**. The past is, as one author put it, more dimly lit than the present. We know a great deal about the first part of the Quaternary Period, Ice Age time, when great continent-wide glaciers covered much of North America and Eurasia and smaller glaciers crept down mountain valleys such as those in Rocky Mountain Park. Most of all, of course, we know about Recent time, the last 10,000 years of the Quaternary Period, when much of the glacial ice melted and *Homo sapiens* came to rule the earth.

So where does Rocky Mountain Park fit in? Nearly all the

rocks in the park, part of the core of Colorado's Front Range, are of Precambrian age. Roughly, they fall into two groups, older Precambrian metamorphic rocks about 1750 million years old, and younger Precambrian intrusive rocks about 1400 to 1450 million years old. (I'll get to rock classification in a moment.) There are also some much younger Tertiary volcanic and intrusive rocks in the northwest corner of the park, and some glacier and stream and lake deposits that are so young they have not had time to turn into rock. And we mustn't forget the exciting new deposits of boulders and sand and mud that have formed since the area became a national park. These last remind us that Old Man Earth, for all his 4.6 billion years, still kicks up his heels, loosing rockfalls and landslides and an occasional flood, just as he has been doing for millions and billions of years.

Outside the national park the geologic time story is different. Both east and west of the park there are rocks of intermediate age — younger than the Precambrian mountain core and older than the Tertiary rocks in the northwest part of the park or the recent glacial, landslide, rockfall, and flood deposits. These other rocks — 300 million to about 90 million years old

Leaving a broad, deep swath of destruction, the Lawn Lake flood built a new alluvial fan at the edge of Horseshoe Park.

(Pennsylvanian to Cretáceous in age) have a lot to tell us about the origins of the national park and the Front Range; we'll get back to them later.

Another thing you should notice on the geologic calendar is that everything is upside down. If we were to write a history of the earth we would have to start at the **bottom** of the page instead of at the top. How crazy these geologists are! Well, stop and think. If rocks are formed, say, on the bottom of the sea, as mud and sand wash into the sea or as skeletons of myriads of tiny shellfish accumulate, and then later other layers of sediment are deposited, it stands to reason that the newer, or younger, layers would lie on top of the older ones — as in the calendar. One of the tenets on which geology is based is the **"law of superposition,"** which says that in an undisturbed sequence of layered rocks, the oldest are at the bottom and the youngest are at the top. The key words in that sentence are **"layered"** and **"undisturbed."** Here in the Rocky Mountains the rocks are mightily disturbed, and very few of them are layered. The volcanic rocks and the stream and glacial and lake

In Precambrian time, fingers of light-colored granite, shaped like a giant crab's claw, forced their way into older gneiss.

5

COMMON ROCKS OF
ROCKY MOUNTAIN NATIONAL PARK

CLASS	ROCK	DESCRIPTION
SEDIMENTARY	Sandstone	Grains of sand cemented together
	Shale (mudstone)	Grains of silt and clay cemented together, often breaking into flat slabs
	Conglomerate	Sand and pebbles deposited as gravel, later cemented together
	Limestone	A sedimentary rock composed of the mineral calcite ($CaCO_3$)
IGNEOUS EXTRUSIVE	Rhyolite	Light-colored, very fine-grained volcanic rock, either lava flows or volcanic ash
	Andesite	Medium dark, fine-grained volcanic rock that commonly contains large feldspar crystals in a fine-grained matrix
IGNEOUS INTRUSIVE	Granite	Common light-colored coarse-grained rock with visible crystals of quartz and feldspar, usually peppered with black mica or hornblende
	Monzonite	Medium-grained rock (commonly with some larger grains) made predominantly of feldspar
	Diorite	Dark gray, fine-grained rock common in dikes and sills
	Gabbro	Very dark crystalline rock
METAMORPHIC	Quartzite	Sandstone so tightly cemented that it breaks through individual sand grains
	Gneiss	Banded or streaky crystalline rock formed from older granite or sandstone
	Schist	Medium-grained rock with abundant parallel mica grains

Of the four main rock categories, intrusive, volcanic, and metamorphic rocks are found within Rocky Mountain Park. Sedimentary rocks occur east and west of the park.

deposits, all of which are relatively young, do lie on top of the much older Precambrian rocks. But among the Precambrian rocks we get into trouble, for both the 1750 million year old and the 1450 million year old rocks are all mixed up. Neither is consistently on top; neither is consistently on the bottom. The catch is that during some major mountain-building disturbance the older Precambrian rocks were intruded by masses of molten rock — the stuff of the younger Precambrian rocks — rising from the earth's interior. If you add things from below, don't expect them to end up on top!

A Few Geologic Basics

The Earth — what we can see of it — is composed of rocks, of water in its several forms, and of atmospheric gases. The science of geology is particularly concerned with the rocks that make up the crust of the Earth, and with their origins, but it considers also the water and atmosphere in that they play important roles in the making of rocks, interact with them once they are made, and come to the forefront in their destruction and removal.

Geologists recognize three main classes of rocks: **igneous, sedimentary**, and **metamorphic**. Since all three classes occur in and near Rocky Mountain National Park, let's look at them in more detail.

Igneous rocks are those formed by the cooling of **magma**, molten rock material, that comes from hot, highly pressurized sources deep within or beneath the Earth's crust. Igneous rocks may cool well below the Earth's surface, in which case they are called **intrusive igneous rocks** — characterized by crystals large enough to be seen by the naked eye. Masses of intrusive igneous rocks — **intrusions** — come in many shapes and sizes, as shown in the diagram. They may push forcibly into older rocks, or they may simply melt their way, assimilating whatever rock they intrude. Fully half of the rocks exposed in Rocky Mountain Park are **granite**, a typically "grainy" (hence its name) intrusive igneous rock. In the park, the younger Precambrian granite, called the Silver Plume Granite, occurs as an immense **batholith** that may in part have melted its way

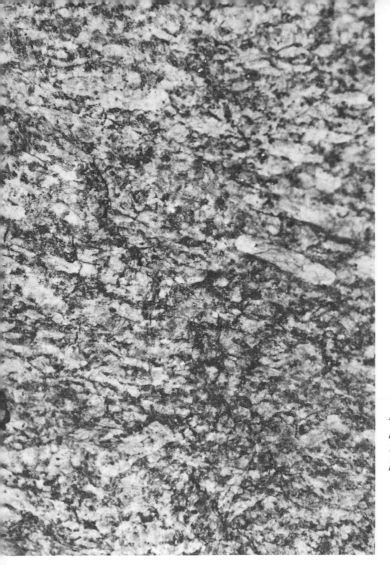

Parallel "laths" of light gray feldspar show that this granite may have flowed as it crystallized.

upward, but in part forced its way into the existing older Precambrian rock as flat **sills**. **Stocks**, smaller than batholiths, occur in the Never Summer Range on the west side of the park, as do some **volcanic plugs**, conduits of long-gone volcanoes. Both are younger than the Precambrian rocks of the rest of the park. Having cooled more rapidly than the ancient granite, they are not as coarsely crystalline, and may have crystals of markedly uneven sizes. **Dikes** occur in many parts of the park; some are Precambrian, some are, like the stocks and plugs, much younger.

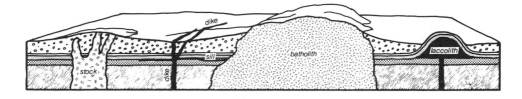

Bodies of intrusive igneous rocks are named according to their size and position relative to other rocks. Intrusive rocks harden below the surface; those shown here are exposed by erosion.

Magma may burst through to the surface to solidify into **extrusive igneous rocks,** more conveniently called **volcanic rocks,** which cool rapidly without time for large crystals to grow. Volcanic rocks — lava flows, volcanic ash deposits called **tuff,** and **volcanic breccia** made of cemented-together fragments of lava and tuff — occur at Specimen Mountain, Lava Cliff, and in the Never Summer Range in the northwest part of the park. Most of these volcanic rocks are **rhyolite**; all are of Tertiary age.

Sedimentary rocks are formed, as their name suggests, from sediments, bits and pieces (like sand, pebbles, and silt) of older rock, or chemically precipitated materials that accumulate on land or in the sea — or for that matter in lakes, ponds, swamps and the like. Some sedimentary rocks are composed of animal and plant remains, notably things like coral skeletons, shells of marine shellfish, or the accumulated plant matter that goes to make up coal. Geologists have standardized their usage of common words like boulder, cobble, gravel, sand, and clay:

> Boulder: diameter greater than 10 inches
> Cobble: diameter 2.5 to 10 inches
> Pebble: diameter 0.2 to 2.5 inches
> Sand: diameter .0025 to 0.2 inches
> Silt: diameter .00016 to .0025 inches
> Clay: finer than .00016 inches

Gravel is a mixture of pebbles, cobbles, and coarse sand. Mud is a mixture of silt and clay.

Most sedimentary rocks were deposited as horizontal layers or strata. Here the strata have been tilted by mountain uplift. W.T. Lee photo, courtesy of USGS.

An important characteristic of most sedimentary rocks is that they are layered or **stratified.** Variations in grain size and changes in rock hardness usually make the layering apparent even from a distance. Stratified Paleozoic and Mesozoic sedimentary rocks are tilted up along both flanks of the Front Range, but they do not reach into the park itself. Cenozoic stream and lake deposits, as well as the rocky, unstratified moraines left by receding glaciers, fit into the sedimentary category even though they are not yet hardened or cemented into rock.

Loose, unconsolidated sediments eventually turn into solid rock. Two or sometimes three processes are at play: As sediments become covered by other sediments or by lava and ash flows they are **compacted** — extra air and water are squeezed out. Groundwater carrying minerals in solution may flow through them, depositing **cements** such as calcium carbonate ($CaCO_3$), iron oxide (Fe_2O_3), or silica (SiO_2), which "glue" individual grains together. Or changes may occur within the sediments themselves, with minerals changing chemically into other minerals, which then may act as cements. Understandably, the degree of compaction or cementation varies with time. Older sedimentary rocks are usually much more tightly compacted and cemented than younger ones.

Metamorphic rocks are previously existing rocks that have been altered by heat and pressure. This category includes the oldest rocks of Rocky Mountain Park: dark gray or silvery

schist with lined-up parallel mica grains, in many cases marked with wavy or knotty streaks of mica or other dark minerals, and **gneiss**, which looks like banded granite.

Metamorphic rocks that have not reached complete recrystallization may still retain many of their original sedimentary or volcanic characteristics. We call such rocks **metasedimentary** or **metavolcanic rocks**. **Quartzite** near the mouth of the Big Thompson Canyon is a metasedimentary rock.

Since they are all composed of crystals large enough to be seen without a lens, gneiss, schist, and granite are frequently lumped together as **crystalline rocks** — a handy catch-all term used frequently in this book.

Rocks of all kinds are made up of **minerals**, natural elements or compounds with definite chemical compositions and usually with characteristic ways of crystallizing — a definition memorized by untold thousands of geology students. One of the most common minerals is **quartz**, which generally occurs as irregular or chunky, glassy crystals in granite and gneiss, as sand grains in sedimentary rock, and as a major component of the white **veins** that lace many crystalline rocks. Quartz is hard enough to scratch both glass and steel.

Large-crystalled pegmatite veins of the same composition as granite penetrate fine-grained older rock.

Other common minerals, which as a group make up about 60 percent of the earth's crust, are the **feldspars**. These translucent white to pink or pale green minerals are characterized by their rectangular or lathlike crystal shape and by the way they break or **cleave** along flat faces that meet each other at about 90-degree angles. Feldspars are found in practically all igneous and metamorphic rocks, sometimes in quite large crystals. Though they may superficially resemble quartz, they can be scratched with a knife. They are brittle and fairly unstable chemically, breaking up easily and altering to clay when they are exposed to weathering processes.

Another group of rock-forming minerals, the **micas**, also break along flat cleavage planes, but in them the planes are parallel and close together so that individual crystals break apart into thin, somewhat flexible flakes. Micas vary in color from clear-as-glass **muscovite** to black or very dark green **biotite**. They are much softer than either quartz or the feldspars — you can scratch them quite easily with a pocket knife. Micas, particularly biotite and muscovite, are common in granite and gneiss and may appear to be almost the sole component of schist.

Granite, gneiss, and schist also may contain minerals of the **amphibole** group, black, brown, or very dark green minerals that usually form thin, rodlike crystals. **Hornblende** is a common mineral of this group.

A pretty skeletal review of rocks and minerals; we'll be fleshing it out as we drive the roads and hike the trails of Rocky Mountain Park.

Geologic Architecture

We're now equipped with a calendar of geologic time and with the names of some rocks and minerals. But before we can build the Rockies we need a few more terms.

Geologists speak of two main structural features of the Earth's crust: **folds** and **faults**. **Folds** are as you might guess bends in the rocks — and they needn't be as neat as the everyday meaning of the term might imply. Folds may be large or small, gentle or tightly compressed. They are most easily identified in layered rocks — sedimentary rocks or layers of vol-

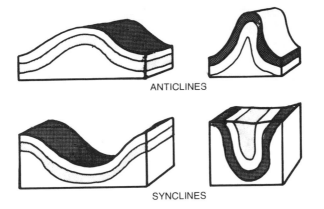

ANTICLINES

SYNCLINES

Folds are easily recognized when they occur in stratified sedimentary or volcanic rocks.

canic lava or ash. They often go unrecognized in granite.

Two main classes of folds, **anticlines** and **synclines**, are best defined by illustration. In anticlines, which are upward folds, the oldest rocks are in the center; in synclines, downward folds, the central rocks are the youngest. In very tight, close-together folds, where rock layers are squeezed together in accordion pleats, the layered sequence may look like unfolded stratified rock, but be much thicker than it originally was.

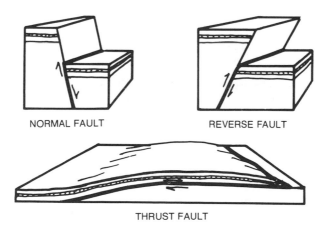

NORMAL FAULT

REVERSE FAULT

THRUST FAULT

Normal, reverse, and thrust faults occur in and near Rocky Mountain Park.

Faults are fractures in rock along which movement has taken place — up-and-down movement or back-and-forth movement of the two sides relative to each other. **Fault planes** — planes of breakage and movement — may be nearly vertical, as shown in the diagram. Faults with steep fault planes are classified as **normal** or **reverse** faults depending on which side goes up and which side goes down. In **thrust faults** the rocks move along nearly horizontal fault planes, with one mass of rock pushed over the other.

There are plenty of faults in the park, probably many more than anyone has counted. Some are really **fault zones** — clusters of more or less parallel faults that weaken the rock enough to control development of valleys and ridges. Others are barely discernible even by careful mapping.

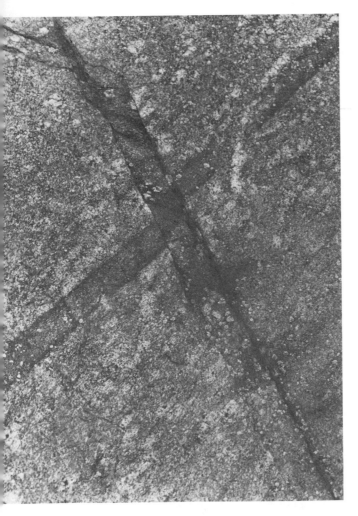

X marks the spot where two small faults offset a slender dike or vein. Without the vein to indicate relative movement, these faults would appear to be joints.

Near Estes Park a granite dome reveals the concentric pressure-release joints that govern its shape.

Joints are, in a way, little faults that didn't move. They are cracks or breaks or fractures in rock along which no discernible movement has taken place. To get a joint at all you have to have some movement of course — the two sides have to move apart at least a little — but the movement is negligible in terms of displacing rocks on one side relative to those on the other. As you've probably noticed already just by looking out your car window, there are plenty of joints in the rocks of Rocky Mountain Park.

Joints are clues to the stresses and hence the forces involved in mountain upheaval. They commonly come in parallel sets — some vertical, some horizontal, some diagonal. More or less concentric pressure-release joints, common in large granite outcrops, are due to expansion of the rocks as pressure is lessened, as when thousands of feet of overlying rocks are eroded away, or as heavy burdens of glacial ice disappear.

In the Front Range there is one gigantic fold, as well as many smaller ones. The giant fold is the range itself — a long, narrow anticline that extends from north of the Wyoming border to the southern slope of Pikes Peak. But as in many other sub-ranges

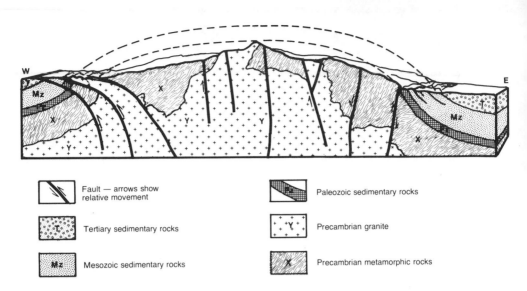

W

E

Fault — arrows show relative movement

Tertiary sedimentary rocks

Mesozoic sedimentary rocks

Paleozoic sedimentary rocks

Precambrian granite

Precambrian metamorphic rocks

Pushed upward at the end of Cretaceous time, the Front Range is edged with major faults. This simplified cross section shows the upturned sedimentary layers worn away along the edges of the Precambrian mountain core.

of the Rocky Mountain chain, the Front Range is faulted as well as folded. Along both edges, the old Precambrian crystalline rocks — rocks that don't fold easily — are broken along giant fault zones with displacement measured not in feet but in miles. Sedimentary rock layers, pushed and dragged upward, in theory stretched and arched in an anticline across the central block. Lay a blanket across some unsecured planking, lift one plank, and you will get the general idea. In geologic parlance, the Front Range is a **faulted anticline.**

Did these sedimentary layers really cover the range like the blanket over the plank? No, probably not. High-gradient streams in mountains run faster than low-gradient streams on plains, and faster streams are better able to cut into mountain flanks and to carry silt and sand or bounce cobbles and boulders down their courses. So erosion began to destroy the mountains even as, little by little, they rose. Understandably, it whittled away at the highest rocks first — the relatively soft sedimentary layers —, breaking them into fragments and carrying the fragments eastward and westward to surrounding lowlands. Long before the mountains reached their present height, the sedimentary rocks on top were gone, leaving only their upturned edges along the margins of the mountain core.

16

Weathering and Erosion

While we're talking about erosion I should mention that there are two distinct processes at play in the wearing down of the mountains.One is **weathering** — the gradual chemical and physical alteration that takes place when rock is exposed to the atmosphere and to surface or near-surface water. Weathering results in changes visible on rock surfaces — changes in color and texture particularly — and in loosening of individual grains or crystals, creating sand and soil. In cold climates and at high altitudes frost plays an important part in breaking rocks apart. Water seeping between grains and into joints freezes at night, melts during the day, and freezes again the next night. Since water expands slightly each time it freezes, grains are eventually loosened and rocks are pried apart along joint planes.

The other half of erosion is **transportation**, whereby loosened rock material is swept away by water, wind, ice, or just plain gravity. Above treeline in the mountains, as you'll see, wind is a particularly important erosional agent — nearly always present, nearly always strong. There, too, ground frost plays an important role in moving particles of soil downhill.

Erosion by water creates stream valleys that are initially V-shaped in cross section, and that can usually be distinguished from more or less U-shaped troughs carved by mountain glaciers. In many cases, though, stream valleys later become flat-floored, partly filled with stream and lake deposits. And the walls of glacial gorges may collapse once the glaciers melt away, with sliding rocks and soil obscuring the earlier U-shaped profile.

Some rocks, such as shale and volcanic ash, erode very easily. Others, like lava flows and beds of well cemented sandstone, resist erosion. So we speak of **differential erosion** whereby softer rocks are washed away while harder, more resistant ones are left relatively untouched. Rock age may play a part in differential erosion: In a very general way, rocks harden with time. The ancient crystalline rocks that core the Front Range, for instance, are exceedingly resistant. Rock structures may also govern differential erosion, with streams able to cut more easily through broken rocks along faults or softer rocks exposed along anticlines or synclines.

The Growth of the Rockies

The story of Rocky Mountain Park began some 1750 million years ago, with metamorphism of the oldest rocks in the park. Earlier, some sort of rocks must have existed, sandstone and shale deposited in a primeval sea, and probably some volcanic rocks, too. Deeply buried, these rocks were so heated and squeezed and broken by mountain-building forces that they became almost unrecognizable as sedimentary or volcanic rock — that they were altered into metamorphic rock, mostly schist.

Some 300 million years after the schist had formed, but still in Precambrian time, molten magma rose from the earth's interior, pushing and melting its way into the older rock. Probably mountains were formed at the time of the intrusion, mountains perhaps like today's Sierra Nevada. We know very little about these mountains, though, for they were worn away by a long, long period of erosion at the end of Precambrian time, leaving only their schist and granite roots.

During the Paleozoic Era the vast lowland that developed during this episode of erosion was at times below and at times above the sea. Sheetlike layers of sedimentary rock — sandstone, shale, and limestone — were deposited in shallow seas that periodically swept onto the continent from the west. Then around 300 million years ago, during Pennsylvanian time, island ancestors of the present Rocky Mountains pushed up from the sea — one of them in almost the position of the present Front Range. Weathering and erosion gradually stripped from these "Ancestral Rockies" their layers of sedimentary rock, and deposited the debris in great apronlike **alluvial fans** along the mountain margins, where it later became the rock known as the Fountain Formation. Through much of the Mesozoic Era the islands continued to wear down, until near the end of Mesozoic time, during the Cretaceous Period, seas once more swept uninterrupted across the region, this time from the east and south.

The present Rocky Mountains came into being at the end of the Mesozoic Era, between 75 and 50 million years ago, during another mountain-building episode. On the larger scale, this mountain-building came about as a result of America's break with Europe, when North America began to drift westward, overriding the Pacific sea floor (a process that is still going on).

The lifting of the present Rockies dragged on for millions of years, with sporadic movement along great faults, with bending and shattering of rocks near the fault zones, and with some folding of sedimentary rocks. Toward the end of the mountain-building episode, molten magma again squeezed up, creating the stocks of the Never Summer Range, as well as many dikes and veins. Now and then magma reached the surface in violent volcanic eruptions.

Even as uplift and intrusion built the mountains, erosion wore them down. Streams and rivers once more deposited their debris on the Great Plains to the east and in intermountain valleys to the west — an unbelievable quantity of boulders, cobbles, pebbles, sand, and silt that left the mountains almost buried in their own debris. By 36 million years ago the Front Range consisted of a narrowed band of rolling uplands that rose only a few thousand feet above their surroundings. Hardly the mountains we see today.

The summits of Stones Peak, left, and Terra Tomah are remnants of the Tertiary upland surface, now raised by regional uplift. National Park Service photo.

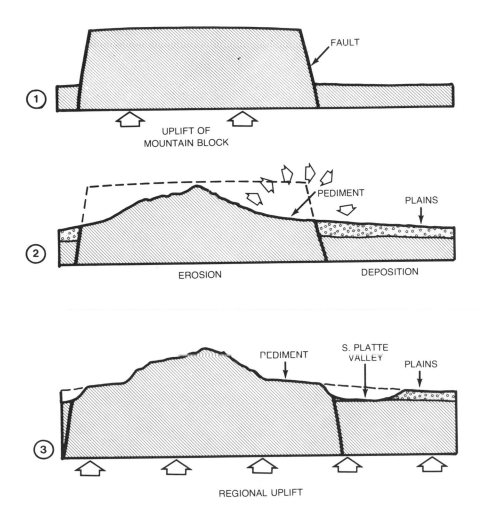

A pediment developed in Tertiary time testifies to two periods of uplift separated by a period of erosion, as shown in these diagrammatic cross sections of the Front Range.

1. The mountain block pushes up in late Cretaceous-early Tertiary time.

2. The mountain block erodes, contributing debris to surrounding plains. Gently sloping pediments develop as the mountains wear back.

3. With regional uplift late in Tertiary time, the South Platte River excavates a broad valley between mountain and plain. Because the mountain core is harder than the new-laid gravels of the plains, the shoulder-like pediment remains, a stairstep between mountain and valley.

20

About 28 million years ago the land began to rise again, this time as part of much broader uplift that involved all of Colorado and Wyoming and large parts of neighboring states. Here in Colorado, lowland plains became 8000 to 9000 feet high, highlands that had been 3000 feet in elevation were raised to 9000 feet or more, and peaks of 8000 feet became Colorado's famous "Fourteeners." Again, uplift prompted erosion. With new vigor the streams attacked not just the mountains, but also the thick, loose aprons of debris on and along their flanks. Stripping away rocks and sand, gravel and clay, streams bared the old mountain core.

In Quaternary time, as frigid climates of the Ice Ages waxed and waned, erosion was sped up by growth of **glaciers** on high mountain peaks. Creeping down pre-existing stream valleys, the rivers of ice scraped and rasped and ground away the rock, freezing to it and pulling fragments loose, excavating deep, straight, troughlike valleys. Later, as the glaciers melted, they left behind new landforms: high, scoop-shaped cirques, rock-rimmed lakes, stairstepped valleys, and the untidy piles of rocky rubble that we call **moraines**: **lateral moraines** at their

Andrews Glacier at the head of Andrews Creek has been shrinking for more than 50 years.
National Park Service photo.

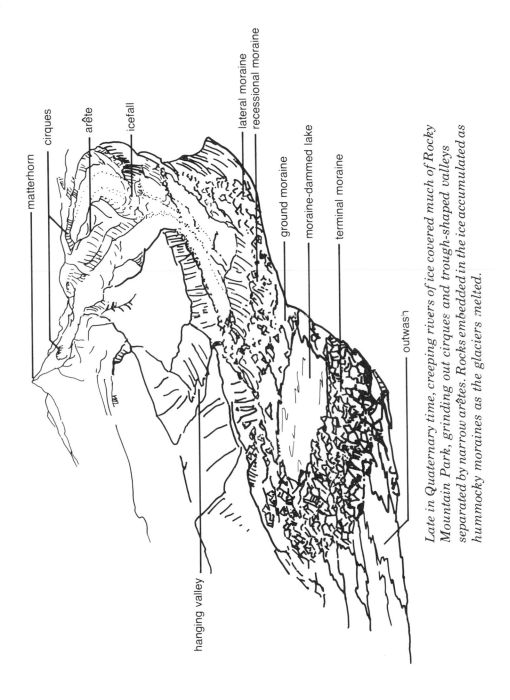

matterhorn

cirques

arête

icefall

lateral moraine

recessional moraine

ground moraine

moraine-dammed lake

terminal moraine

outwash

hanging valley

Late in Quaternary time, creeping rivers of ice covered much of Rocky Mountain Park, grinding out cirques and trough-shaped valleys separated by narrow arêtes. Rocks embedded in the ice accumulated as hummocky moraines as the glaciers melted.

sides, **terminal moraines** at their lower ends, and **recessional moraines** across the tips of receding glaciers.

In this part of the Rockies there is evidence of three glacial advances and retreats. The oldest of the three — the most extensive — left the lowest moraines, deeply weathered and now hardly recognizable. The second advance left moraines that are still distinct: pronounced rocky, forested ridges with gray-brown soil. The third advance left moraines characterized now by sandy soil and fresh-looking boulders. In the warming climate that followed the last advance, the glaciers melted away completely.

But there **are** glaciers now in Rocky Mountain Park, small ones nestling in high cirques along the Continental Divide. They are thought to result from a "Little Ice Age" that climaxed about 4000 years ago. At present they are shrinking. Will they continue to do so? Or is their presence a harbinger of another glacial cycle to come?

With that chilly thought, it is high time to go out and look at some geology. Chapter II covers roadside geology along four approaches to the park. Chapter III is concerned with roads within the park. Chapter IV deals with eight hiking trails and geologic features to be seen along them.

U.S. Highway 36 drops into Estes Park, a wide mountain valley framed in granite hills and snow-capped peaks.

II.
Roadside Geology: Getting to the Park

U.S. 36
Lyons to Rocky Mountain National Park
(Deer Ridge)

Lyons owes its existence, in part, to the salmon-colored Lyons Sandstone that is quarried nearby for use as ornamental building stone. As the island mountains of the Ancestral Rockies of Pennsylvanian time wore down, their own debris piled up around them, forming a coastal plain. On this wind-swept plain, between the mountains and the sea, sand dunes formed in Permian time, dunes much like those we encounter along today's sea and lake shorelines. Eventually, the dune sands became the Lyons Sandstone, a rock that breaks into smooth, flat flagstones along diagonal planes that mark the leeward slopes of the dunes. The large scale of this diagonal **crossbedding**, as well as the fine, even-grained nature of the sandstone itself, identifies these rocks as dune-formed sandstone.

The Lyons Formation appears in highway cuts north of the T junction in Lyons. The quarries are in the broad swale north of the town. Like other sedimentary rocks along the mountain front, the formation slants upward toward the mountain core.

The rock that lies beneath the Lyons Sandstone, the Fountain Formation, appears between mileposts (mps) 20 and 19. It, too, tilts up toward the mountains. The dark pink sandstone layers of this formation in places contain stream-rounded pebbles. The sandstone layers alternate with fine, chippy, dark red

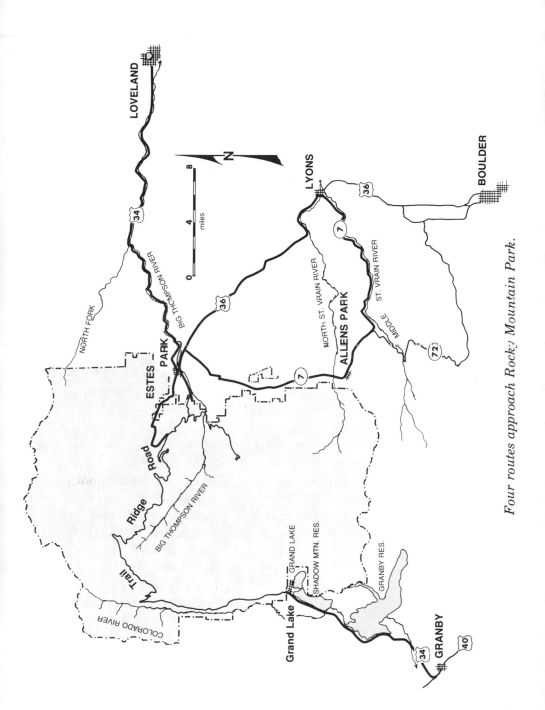

Four routes approach Rocky Mountain Park.

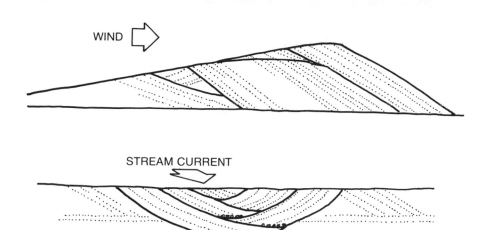

Ancient sedimentary environments can often be recognized by analogy with modern sediments. The Lyons Sandstone bears long, sweeping crossbedding like that in modern dunes. In the Fountain Formation, festoon-like crossbedding compares with that of modern stream channels.

mudstone. These are the rocks of the alluvial fans and coastal plain on which the Lyons sand dunes developed. They display another type of crossbedding, the festoon or channel type that develops as streams shift and abandon their former channels.

Near mp 18 the highway curves westward across a little valley and approaches the mountains proper. The contact between the Pennsylvanian Fountain Formation and the Precambrian granite of the mountain core lies along this valley. Here and elsewhere the contact involves a deeply weathered granite surface — a sign of long-drawn-out exposure to the atmosphere. The deep weathering, the absence of sedimentary rocks older than the Fountain Formation, and the coarseness of the Fountain Formation itself are all lines of evidence by which geologists have deduced the existence of the Ancestral Rocky Mountains of Pennsylvanian and Permian time.

The reddish gray granite of the Front Range core, eroded into knobby hills and steep cliffs, weathers to a brownish gray. There are lots of good roadcut exposures of the unweathered rock, shiny with feldspar and mica. Several sets of parallel joints slice through the rock. Pressure-release joints, more or less concentric with today's surface, are due to the rock's expansion as its overburden — all the rock that was once above it — was worn away.

The road at first stays near the North St. Vrain River, twisting and turning up a canyon that is, overall, V-shaped in its cross-profile — the work of running water.

Other types of rock appear between mps 16 and 14: fine-grained schist with gnarled bands of light and dark minerals, cut by narrow veins of quartz and wider granite dikes. North of mp 14 we come into granite again. All along here there are convenient turn-outs if you want to stop for a closer look.

The mountain community of Pinewood Springs lies in a pocket of deeply weathered granite, with the weathering dating back perhaps to Tertiary time. As you can easily recognize, the valley has much thicker soils than the hills that surround it, where rounded granite knobs appear at the surface.

North of mp 11 some darker gray granite shows a natural tendency to break along regularly spaced vertical joints — a characteristic utilized by roadbuilders, with the result that joint surfaces are now well exposed. Some are coated with thin veneers of dark reddish brown **hematite** or yellower **limonite** — the familiar iron oxides of rust — derived from iron-bearing minerals such as biotite. Roadcuts across from the big parking area at mp 8 display rock types that include granite, gneiss, and schist, as well as **pegmatite**, a granite-like rock containing crystals of glassy quartz, pink feldspar, and white mica an inch or more in diameter. Just north of mp 8, on the west side of the road, are two masses of **diorite**, gray intrusive rock dark with minerals of the amphibole group. Diorite is quite common in dikes and sills.

Another meadowed mountain valley lies north of mp 6. In such roadcuts as there are here, the granite is again deeply weathered, just about falling apart into sand. For such highly weathered "rotten granite" geologists use the German word **grus.**

Just north of mp 4 the road tops a drainage divide and starts its descent into Estes Park, one of the largest valleys along the east slope of the Front Range. From the viewpoint a short distance north of mp 3, the valley shows in its entirety, from the narrow river passage at its upper end, west of the town of Estes Park, to Olympus Dam at its lower end. The wide valley, at the confluence of the Big Thompson and Fall Rivers, lies at the junction of three large faults, features that may have assisted in valley widening. Although the valley may seem U-shaped, Ice Age glaciers did not reach it. Its floor is, however, filled in

Lumpy Ridge with its rounded granite knobs rises above Lake Estes.

with **glacial outwash,** coarse, bouldery gravels washed in by meltwater streams from the glaciers.

Beyond Estes Park, and easily recognized by its descriptive name, is Lumpy Ridge. As you might suspect it gets its name from the granite outcrops along its summit.

Before leaving this viewpoint take a close look at the rock in the highway cut opposite. Notice how clusters of dark amphibole minerals are surrounded by lighter areas. Because the white-surrounded clusters resemble eyes ("augen" in German), this rock is called **augen gneiss.**

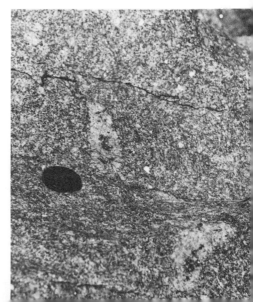

Two stony "eyes" gaze from augen gneiss. Camera cap is 2 inches in diameter.

U.S. 36 drops down to Lake Estes and passes close to the power plant at its west end. Visitors are welcome at this plant, which produces hydroelectric power with water that comes by a 13-mile tunnel under Rocky Mountain National Park, from Grand Lake on the western slope of the range. Lake Estes is about a thousand feet lower than Grand Lake, giving the water the "head" necessary for power production. An interesting facet of the Big Thompson water and power project is that water travels from west to east and electric power from east to west, both through the same tunnel!

The highway runs through downtown Estes Park and turns left in the center of town. It then circles the hilly south part of town and continues on to Rocky Mountain Park. Park headquarters and a visitor center, where you may attend an introductory program and look at a relief map of the park, are to your left a short distance west of the park boundary.

Beyond the entrance station, the Moraine Park-Bear Lake Road branches off to the south, leading to one of the most spectacular parts of the park. There, many trails lead up into glaciated valleys (see Chapters III and IV).

Beaver Meadows, near the entrance station, is 8000 feet in elevation, normally the lower limit of Ice Age glaciation in this part of Colorado. Yet it has not been glaciated: No cirques mark the head of the valley; no terminal moraines dam its lower end. It owes its existence to a glacier that came down the valley of the Big Thompson River, in the next drainage to the south. The north lateral moraine of the Big Thompson glacier forms the long, straight-topped hill south of Beaver Meadows.

The highway zigzags up out of Beaver Meadows and onto Deer Ridge, where it joins U.S. 34 to become Trail Ridge Road, discussed in Chapter III.

U.S. 34 Loveland to Rocky Mountain National Park

Loveland lies on Cretaceous rocks — dark gray marine shale, soft and easily weathered sedimentary rock that develops into good agricultural soil. Between the town and the mountains these layered rocks, as well as older rocks that underlie them, were dragged upward by the rising mountains. Then they were partly eroded away. The more resistant rock layers, nicely emphasized by differential erosion, show up along the highway west of town.

At milepost (mp) 89 the highway passes through the first ridge of resistant rock — the Dakota Sandstone. This is a beach sandstone laid down as Cretaceous seas swept into this area from the southeast about 100 million years ago. From Wyoming to New Mexico an outcrop of this once flat-lying but now tilted rock, the Dakota Hogback, runs along the edge of the mountains in an almost unbroken line.

Here west of Loveland there is a disruption in that line — a double fold that brings the Dakota Sandstone upward, downward, and upward again, so that its trace on the ground (and on the geologic map) comes out in a sharp Z pattern. The ridge at mp 89 is the first sign of this double fold. Rocks east of the ridge are younger than the Dakota Sandstone; those west of it are older.

Closer to the mountains the Dakota Sandstone plunges abruptly, essentially vertically, down through the surface again, as do its neighboring rocks. To some extent this vertical part of the double fold is also faulted. Erosion of the fold has left the resistant Dakota Sandstone standing as picturesque Devils Backbone.

Rocks in the narrow valley east of the Backbone are older than the Dakota: Triassic and Jurassic sandstones and shales. Those west of it are younger — the soft Pierre Shale, the same rock that underlies Loveland.

Having bent up and then down, the Dakota Sandstone must bend up again, reflecting the upward drag of the mountains. This it does between mp 87, at the first bridge over the Big Thompson River, and mp 86, near the second bridge. Notice that the river is deflected southward around the Devils Backbone.

West of this third exposure of the Dakota Sandstone, sedimentary layers once again are older: the Jurassic Morrison Formation mudstone forming a broad, fertile swale, and west of mp 86 the salmon-colored Lyons Sandstone, resistant enough to form another hogback ridge. Of Permian age, the Lyons Sandstone originated as sand dunes between the sea to the east and the eroding Ancestral Rockies to the west. You can still see the long, slanting **crossbedding** created as fine, rounded sand grains, carried by wind up gentle windward dune slopes, settled on the steep leeward faces.

West of the Lyons Sandstone ridge are darker red and white siltstone, sandstone, and **conglomerate** layers that make up the Fountain Formation, a rock unit that accumulated as sand, pebbles, and silt washed off the Ancestral Rockies in late Pennsylvanian time, some 300 million years ago. These rocks are exposed near the highway and along the river in the last stretch before the mountains.

The front of the Front Range rises abruptly. A change of rock type is immediately apparent. Hard, dark, resistant rocks, standing on end like books on a shelf, wall in the Big Thompson River. These metasedimentary rocks, altered sedimentary rocks some 1.75 billion years old, consist of quartzite (once sandstone) and slaty schist (once mudstone or shale). The river has sliced an especially narrow canyon where they are lined up parallel to its route.

Wrapped around a boulder by the force of the stream, this is one of 197 automobiles demolished by the Big Thompson flood in August, 1976.
R.R. Shroba photo, courtesy of USGS.

The flood destroyed many homes and cottages near the river and along its floodplain.

In August 1976 the Big Thompson Canyon was a scene of destruction and disaster. Upstream, near and north of Estes Park, extremely heavy rains caused a sudden rise in the level of the Big Thompson River. As the flood swept downstream, the water level in the Narrows, (where it didn't even rain!) rose as much as 40 feet. In all, 140 people died — many of them while trying to outrace the rising waters by car. (The rule for floods — whether you are in a car or not: *Climb: get as high above the river as you can as fast as you can.* Abandon your car — you can't buy a new life.) Much of the highway was demolished, particularly in the Narrows. Several small dams were also swept away. An interesting measure of flood damage is in a small picnic area just east of mp 81, where the bark of a cottonwood tree was stripped away on its upstream side. Along upper parts of the canyon many large old ponderosa pines suffered the same fate; most of them later died.

West of this picnic area the canyon follows a line of weakened rock along the Thompson Canyon Fault Zone. Evidence of flood damage increases. Cutaway banks rise above huge boulders rounded by bouncing and jolting down the flooding stream. Houses on the river floodplain have been built, rebuilt, or extensively repaired since the flood. Memory of the terror in the night and the tumultuous power of the floodwaters has been surprisingly short-lived.

Veins of coarse-grained pegmatite mark many canyon walls. The magma penetrated joints and fissures in much older schist and gneiss.

Farther upstream, rounded slopes knobby with outcrops of purple-gray granite replace the craggy pinnacles of metasedimentary rock of the lower canyon. The granite is interspersed with bands and irregular masses of shiny mica schist, which weathers relatively easily and rarely stands as vertical cliffs. Resistant quartzite and slaty schist, where they occur, are no longer in vertical position as in the Narrows.

Stop and look more closely at the schist near mp 78. Mica makes up a large part of the rock. Its flat flakes, parallel to one another, give the rock its silvery sheen. Intruded into the schist are narrow bands of pink granite and coarse-grained **pegmatite**, a granitelike rock containing quartz, feldspar, and mica crystals several inches in diameter — a magnified version of granite.

Idlewilde Dam furnishes hydroelectric power for the City of Loveland. A resistant granite dike constricts the canyon and forms a convenient dam site.

Between mp 76 and 75 a branch road to the right goes up the North Fork of the Big Thompson River to Glenhaven, in a straight-line route continuing along the Thompson Canyon Fault. Since stream level in both forks rose during the 1976 flood, the little community of Drake, at their confluence, caught trouble from two directions at once.

There is more granite above Drake, some of it very coarse-grained and artistically patterned with sinuous veins. Flood damage was heavy here, too, with the stream cutting most strongly at the outer edges of its curving loops, where stream flow is always fastest. Scars left by caving along the banks will remain evident for years. And the streambed contains boulders much too large to be moved by the stream's normal flow.

West of Drake, schist and granite seem patched and interwoven in complex patterns. Many coarse-grained pegmatite veins cut across the pattern, adding more complexity. Dark, fine-grained veins are **diorite,** an intrusive rock containing dark minerals such as hornblende, along with feldspar and a little

Here, large masses of granite squeezed upward into finely layered schist. Both granite and schist are Precambrian.

Scott W. Starratt
Dept. of Paleontology
U. C. Berkeley
Berkeley, Ca. 94720

quartz. All these rocks are well exposed in highway cuts. Straight stretches of stream and highway follow fault zones or parallel joint sets.

Canyon walls open out west of mp 68, with increasing amounts of granite on surrounding hills. Olympus Dam, at the lower end of the mountain valley of Estes Park, holds water that comes from the other side of the mountains, western slope water intended by nature to flow toward the Pacific. The water comes through the Adams Tunnel from Grand Lake, traveling under Rocky Mountain National Park to Lake Estes. From Prospect Mountain, just across Lake Estes, three conduits bring the water to a hydroelectric plant near the lake. Tunnel intakes on the west side of the mountains are about a thousand feet higher than this power plant, giving the water plenty of "head" for power production. The electricity produced here serves both sides of the divide, for some of it is transmitted westward through the same conduit that brings the water eastward.

From mp 54 the view south across the lake includes the jagged top of Twin Sisters and farther to the west the distant mass of Longs Peak, at 14,255 feet the highest peak in the national park and in this part of the Front Range.

North of the spacious mountain valley of Estes Park is Lumpy Ridge, named for the many granite domes that thrust above the trees. Concentric pressure-release joints in the granite form natural pathways for rain and snowmelt seeping into the rock, and repeated freezing and thawing of water in these joints loosens the weakened rock until curving, scablike layers fall away. Surface weathering and breakdown of mica and feldspar grains help to round the rock surfaces.

Floored with stream-carried glacial outwash from upstream Ice-Age glaciers and with sand and gravel from surrounding ridges, this valley is lower than the 8000-foot lower limit of glaciation in this part of the Rockies, so it was never re-sculptured by glaciers.

Highway 34 circles north around Estes Park, with more good views of the weathered granite of Lumpy Ridge. Passing through the Fall River Narrows, it enters the national park at the Fall River Entrance Station. In the last half mile before the entrance station, roadcuts expose interwoven mixtures of schist and granite called **migmatite**, as well as veins of gray diorite and white quartz. South of the road the Fall River cuts

This great boulder, buried within a moraine at the lower end of Horseshoe Park, was exposed by raging waters of the Lawn Lake flood. Above the old soil line, weathering has altered the longer-exposed rock.

through two terminal moraines, crescents of rocks and sand that delineate the farthest advance of the glaciers. A recessional moraine, younger and much less weathered, curves across Horseshoe Park just west of the highway.

The wide floor of this park represents the extent of former lakes dammed by the terminal moraines. The lakes gradually filled in with stream sediments and plant material; only a few small ponds remain. The youngest of the stream sediments, at the time of this writing, arrived on July 15, 1982, when a breaking dam high up the tributary stream of Roaring River abruptly released the waters of Lawn Lake (see Trail Ridge Road in Chapter III and Lawn Lake Trail in Chapter IV).

From Horseshoe Park the glacier-carved, U-shaped upper canyon of Fall River can be seen to the west. The Old Fall River Road, first park road to cross the mountains, goes up this valley; a roadlog is in Chapter III.

Two small ponds are all that is left of a moraine-dammed lake in Horseshoe Park. Fall River twists across the flat valley floor; light-colored gravels along its banks were deposited by the Lawn Lake flood.

Crossing Fall River, Highway 34 climbs the south lateral moraine of the Fall River Glacier to the crest of Deer Ridge, where it is joined by US 36. It continues west from this junction as Trail Ridge Road, also described in Chapter III.

Highway U.S. 34
Granby to Rocky Mountain National Park

Granby nestles between the Front Range to the east, the Williams Fork Range to the southwest, and the Never Summer Range to the northwest. High hills of light-colored Tertiary sandstone rise up close to the town. Horizontal mesas to the north consist of rounded cobbles and bouldery gravels washed here by streams of meltwater bursting from glaciers that once occupied the upper valley of the Colorado River, Kawuneeche Valley in Rocky Mountain National Park.

Because of all the faults in this area — including a pair of them that run the length of Kawuneeche Valley — the geology on this side of the Front Range has been hard to decipher. Only by carefully mapping rocks of different ages have geologists been able to straighten out the geologic picture.

On this side of the mountains, Cretaceous and older sedimentary rocks do not simply bend up along the base of the Front Range as they do east of the mountains. Precambrian crystalline rocks that core the Front Range have pushed westward over the Cretaceous rocks, which in turn are thrust westward over Tertiary rocks, so that the normal youngest-on-top sequence is reversed. The picture is complicated by many normal faults. And lastly, the thrust slices are in many places eroded away or buried by Tertiary sedimentary and volcanic rocks and by stream and glacial deposits of Quaternary age.

North of Granby the highway enters some of the Cretaceous and Tertiary rocks, approximately following the course of the Colorado River — here of course quite small. At milepost (mp) 4 you can look up the river's V-shaped canyon — its V profile a cue to stream erosion — to the massive slopes of the Front Range. Quite abruptly near mp 7 the route comes into ancient crystalline rocks — Precambrian gneiss, schist, and granite of the Front Range core — pushed westward over younger rocks.

Flowing with little gradient through Kawuneeche Valley, the Colorado River swings lazily in broad meanders. During occasional floods it spreads new layers of sand and gravel across its bordering floodplain.

Light-colored rocks west of the road are mostly volcanic tuff of Tertiary age. At mile 7.8 a lava-capped ridge can be seen ahead.

Between mps 8 and 9 there are good views southeastward to the craggy high country of the Indian Peaks Wilderness Area south of Rocky Mountain National Park. The highway skirts the west shore of Granby Reservoir, with thick, light-colored Tertiary gravel deposits just west of the road. Nearby, Precambrian granite in one of the thrust fault slices weathers as rounded knobs and boulders — a typical weathering form for granite.

Colorado's major population centers lie east of the Front Range in the Fort Collins-Denver-Colorado Springs urban corridor. Precipitation, however, is greater on the western side of the range. Granby Reservoir impounds the waters of the Colorado River and several of its mountain tributaries for transfer to the eastern slope. Water from the reservoir is pumped up into the Granby Pump Canal, which carries it to Shadow Mountain Reservoir and Grand Lake. From there it passes through 13-mile Adams Tunnel under Rocky Mountain National Park to the eastern slope of the Rockies.

Stream-rounded cobbles, pebbles, and sand between mps 11 and 12 were washed here by rushing meltwater streams emerging from Ice Age glaciers. Glacial outwash deposits such as this differ from glacial moraines in two important characteristics: Bouncing along in fast-flowing streams, their rock fragments are rounded by stream abrasion. And the rock fragments are stratified, sorted according to size, with finer and coarser material arranged in layers.

Near the Grand Lake junction the highway passes through the rocky rubble of a moraine. The large boulder at the left is a glacial erratic.
National Park Service photo.

Approaching Shadow Mountain Reservoir the highway crosses several terminal moraines that arch around the south end of Shadow Mountain Reservoir as a succession of islands (easily visible from a picnic area on County Road 66). Terminal moraines are hilly or hummocky and usually crescent-shaped. Like most moraines these are dotted with angular ice-transported boulders.

There is another moraine very near the town of Grand Lake. Roadcut exposures show how unsorted this glacial material is — a mixture of mud, sand, cobbles, and boulders with no sign of layering or stratification.

Of the three lakes here — Granby and Shadow Mountain Reservoirs and Grand Lake — the last is the only completely natural one. Its dam is a big lateral moraine that formed along one side of the Kawuneeche Valley glacier, probably with some contribution from smaller glaciers coming down North Inlet and East Inlet, the two canyons that empty into Grand Lake.

North of the Grand Lake turnoff the highway climbs across the old lateral moraine, and shortly after that enters the national park. For a continuation of this log see Trail Ridge Road in Chapter III.

Grand Lake, just in sight to the left, is separated from Shadow Mountain Reservoir by the lateral moraine of the Kawuneeche Valley glacier. National Park Service photo.

CO 7 Lyons to Estes Park

An attractive approach to Estes Park and Rocky Mountain National Park, this route follows the South St. Vrain River upstream from Lyons. It leaves Lyons through tilted sedimentary rocks of the Fountain Formation, rocks which underlie the salmon-colored Lyons Sandstone, quarried for use as ornamental building stone.

The Fountain Formation's layers consist of pink and grayish purple conglomerate, sandstone, and mudstone. They were deposited in alluvial fans and on a coastal plain that bordered the eastern front of the Ancestral Rockies of Pennsylvanian time. The formation is well exposed in roadcuts and natural outcrops along and above the highway. All of the layers were tilted by the rise of the present Front Range in late Cretaceous time. White bands in these rocks are zones in which iron oxides, which give the surrounding rock its brick-red color, have been leached away by groundwater filtering through narrow joints and along contacts between sandstone and mudstone layers.

Among the varied rock types of the Fountain Formation, the sandstone layers are most resistant. Rounded ledges of sandstone can be seen on slopes north of the highway between mileposts (mps) 31 and 30. The same rocks are present south of the river, but there some igneous rocks occurs, too, in a sill that

41

forced its way, when molten, between the sedimentary layers. This sill and the pink rocks adjacent to it are quarried for gravel, riprap, and other uses. Stop in sight of the quarry, west of mp 31, to look at the **columnar joints** in the sill, which formed as the molten rock cooled, crystallized, and shrank. The sill follows first one sandstone layer and then another. As it bends between layers, the columnar joints remain perpendicular to the original cooling surfaces — the upper and lower margins of the sill.

The contact of the Fountain Formation with Precambrian granite of the Front Range core is close to the Roosevelt National Forest boundary sign. Though the actual contact is covered with old stream deposits and present-day soils, we know there are no pre-Fountain Formation sedimentary rocks here, for when the Ancestral Rocky Mountains rose in Pennsylvanian time all the earlier sedimentary layers were eroded from the island range. The granite-cored island was then beveled and deeply weathered before the Fountain Formation was deposited along its eastern flank.

Dark pinkish gray granite of this part of the mountain core contains chunky crystals of quartz, hornblende, and mica, as well as long white or glassy laths of feldspar. The feldspar laths in many cases lie parallel to each other, indicating that the granite still flowed a little as it crystallized. In natural exposures the granite is streaked with black lichens growing along seepage zones.

Joints are abundant. Some are vertical or nearly so, and were caused by stresses and strains as the Earth's crust moved and bent. Curving cracks more or less concentric with the surface are pressure-release joints formed when the immense pressures existing within the granite were lessened by erosion of the overburden.

The granite country is steep and rugged. South St. Vrain River has cut a deep, twisting canyon with a V-shaped cross profile. Canyon walls are the sites of numerous **talus** slopes and of landslides of crushed and broken rock fragments mixed with sand and soil.

The river has also polished many of the rocks that wall its channel, abrading them with sand carried in the water. In places the rushing water has excavated **potholes** by whirling loose rocks in whirlpools. There are many spots along this road where you can stop for a closer look at the granite and at features formed by stream processes. Try to find fresh faces of the pink or purple granite, and notice the differences between these faces and weathered surfaces. In roadcuts, note the drill holes for dynamite, some surrounded by stars of shattered rock. Some of the granite contains lens-shaped aggregates of dark mica crystals.

Criss crossing joints are well exposed on the rock face across the stream from mp 26. Farther upstream, several east-facing granite surfaces shine with **slickensides** — the smooth, polished rock "skin" that results from the grinding of rock against rock along faults. Because there is no layering in this rock, it's hard to tell where faults are; slickensides are often the only indication of movement. Here as in most fault zones movement is taken up along several parallel surfaces.

West of mp 25 watch for an abrupt change in rock type. A wide dark gray dike appears at roadside, composed of fine-grained diorite. Nearby are several masses of **pegmatite** — like granite in composition, but much coarser in grain size. A short distance east of the dike is another slickensided fault surface, this one gently waving. There are more of these fault surfaces farther up the road.

At mile 24 the highway touches the northeastern tip of the Colorado Mineral Belt, a broad southwest-trending zone in which is found most of the state's mineral wealth. A few prospect holes, some small mine dumps, and the foundations of an old mill clue us in to mining activity here. Small ore bodies lie along joints and faults in Precambrian rock, but mineral enrichment probably took place in Tertiary time. The mineralized area continues to the Raymond junction and beyond. Raymond was originally a mining town.

At mp 20, near the Raymond junction, we come on some metamorphic rocks, representatives of the other main rock group of Rocky Mountain National Park. Bands of schist and wandering veins of coarse pegmatite mingle here with the granite.

Glacier View overlook provides a distant view of Isabelle Glacier in the Indian Peaks Wilderness Area. Hardly more than a patch of snow from this distance, this is one of several small glaciers that lie just east of the crest of the Front Range. The skyline ridge north and south of the glacier is the Continental Divide, the boundary line between streams and rivers that drain ultimately into the Atlantic and those that drain into the Pacific.

At mp 19, Mt. Meeker is in view ahead, its tapered 13,911-foot summit hiding the higher summit of Longs Peak. Both Mt. Meeker and Longs Peak are in Rocky Mountain National Park. The highway route now crosses the Tertiary **pediment,** an irregular, gently sloping stairstep on the mountain front, about 8,000 to 10,000 feet in elevation. This pediment, eroded into the new-formed mountain mass early in Tertiary time, once connected smoothly with the High Plains to the east. The pediment surface is deeply patterned with canyons and valleys cut by the various streams that come off the high mountains to the west. One of the deepest of these valleys is that of the North St. Vrain River. Upstream, the North St. Vrain flows from Wild Basin, within the national park.

As CO 7 climbs out of the valley of the North St. Vrain, the rocky ridge and double summit of Twin Sisters appear straight ahead, their rugged slopes of schist and gneiss rising above the Tertiary pediment. Tahosa Valley, between Twin Sisters and Mt. Meeker, is edged on the west with hilly glacial deposits, some of which come quite near the highway.

Near mp 9 a branch road leads to Longs Peak Campground and the trailhead for the Longs Peak and Chasm Lake trails

A beaver pond and lodge in Tahosa Valley remind us that mountain lakes gradually fill in to become meadows. National Park Service photo.

Forested moraines outline the former extent of Mills Glacier, which flowed from the great cirque below Longs Peak. Shadowed cliff is the "Diamond."
Jack Rathbone photo.

(described in Chapter IV). The best views of Longs Peak from the highway are from open meadows near mp 8. There are also good views from the Twin Sisters trail, reached from the trailhead at mp 8. The near-vertical east face of Longs Peak, the rockclimbers' famous "Diamond," is the headwall of a deep cirque that lies cradled between the arms of Mt. Lady Washington on the north and Mt. Meeker on the south. Chasm Lake lies within this cirque, out of sight from the highway. Thickly forested lateral and terminal moraines of the glacier that carved this cirque reach down toward Tahosa Valley from the slopes of Mt. Meeker and Mt. Lady Washington.

Between mps 8 and 7 the highway crosses Wind River Pass, where it leaves Tahosa Valley and enters the drainage of the Big Thompson River. The mountain valley of Estes Park soon comes into view — a major valley excavated in the Tertiary pediment.

Nearby Marys Lake, as well as Lake Estes in the bottom of the valley, are staging points on the Colorado-Big Thompson Project — a project that brings western slope water through the Adams tunnel beneath Rocky Mountain National Park, to the thickly populated region east of the mountains. Flowing down-hill from Grand Lake and Shadow Mountain Reservoir on the west side of the mountains, this water is also used to produce hydroelectric power. The power plant, near the junction with U.S. 36, welcomes visitors.

To reach Rocky Mountain Park from this junction, follow either U.S. 36 or U.S. 34.

The Bear Lake Road opens up vistas of high peaks along the Continental Divide. Hallett Peak and Flattop Mountain border a glaciated valley accessible only by trail.

Scott W. Starratt
Dept. of Paleontology
U. C. Berkeley
Berkeley, Ca. 94720

III.
Roadside Geology:
Park Roads

Trail Ridge Road (U.S. 34/36)

This route may be traveled in either direction. Use your car odometer, as there are no mileposts on park roads. Recommended stops are printed in **bold type**.

Westbound		Eastbound
0.0	**Park Headquarters, visitor center**	**43.6**

A short slide or film program and a relief map at this visitor center introduce visitors to the national park.

3.8	**Viewpoint with exhibits**	**39.8**

Beaver Meadows, below this vista point, at first glance appears similar to glacial valleys in other parts of the park. The mountain slopes that drain into this valley, however, show no signs of glaciation — just smooth, tree-covered slopes formed by stream erosion. Nevertheless, the little valley is a product of glaciation. Large glaciers flowing down Forest Canyon into Moraine Park, south of Beaver Meadows, left long, straight-topped lateral moraines, one of which effectively closed off this valley. You can see Moraine Park's two thickly forested lateral moraines from this viewpoint.

Behind them, beyond more forested slopes, rises Longs Peak.

47

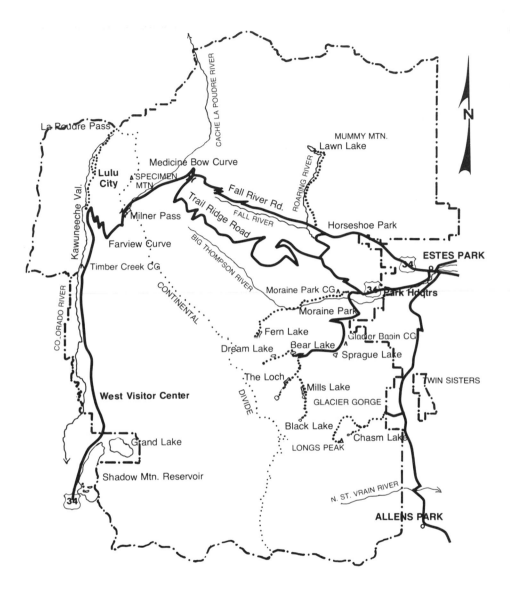

Rocky Mountain National Park, showing park roads and trails described in this guide.

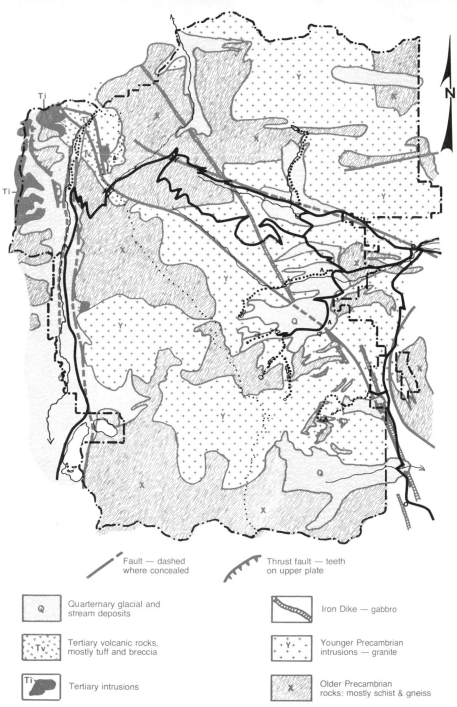

Fault — dashed
where concealed

Thrust fault — teeth
on upper plate

Q — Quarternary glacial and
stream deposits

Iron Dike — gabbro

Tv — Tertiary volcanic rocks,
mostly tuff and breccia

Y — Younger Precambrian
intrusions — granite

Ti — Tertiary intrusions

X — Older Precambrian
rocks: mostly schist & gneiss

A geologic map shows what rocks appear at the surface or just below a thin soil layer. This one gives a generalized view of rock types and ages in Rocky Mountain Park.

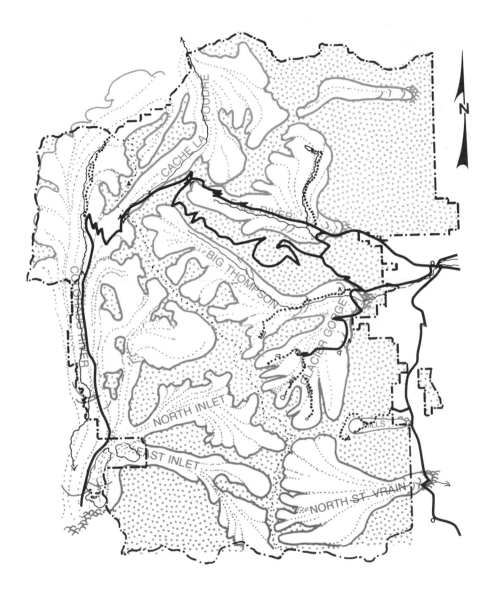

During the last Ice Age, slow-moving rivers of ice covered much of Rocky Mountain Park. When the glaciers melted they left a legacy of high, cup-shaped cirques, troughlike valleys, glacial grooves and striae, and hilly moraines.

At 14,255 feet it is by far the giant of the park. The peak itself is composed of massive, resistant Precambrian granite. Summits and saddles to the right of Longs Peak mark the Continental Divide. Streams draining their eastern slopes flow ultimately into the Atlantic; those draining their western slopes flow to the Pacific.

4.5	**Deer Ridge, Jct with US 34**	**39.1**

Take a moment to enjoy the magnificent views from Deer Ridge — northward across Horseshoe Park and Fall River to the Mummy Range, southward to flat-topped Longs Peak, and southwestward to the glacier-carved peaks and saddles along the divide. Individual peaks are identified in exhibits at Moraine Park Visitor Center and at Forest Canyon Overlook on Trail Ridge Road.

Brought closer by a telephoto lens, Longs Peak rises above the straight-topped lateral moraines that border Moraine Park. National Park Service photo.

The slender, straight-topped lateral moraine of the Fall River glacier separates Hidden Valley (foreground) from the grassy meadows of Horseshoe Park. National Park Service photo.

5.3-6.8   **Hidden Valley**   **36.8-38.3**

Hidden from Horseshoe Park by the lateral moraine of the Fall River glacier, this narrow valley now holds Hidden Valley Creek and the beaver ponds along it. As the ponds fill with silt and plant growth, they will develop into meadows; several stages in this process can be seen here.

8.0   **Lawn Lake Flood viewpoint**   **35.6**

Glacial features of Horseshoe Park took second place in 1982 to the sudden development of new landforms brought about by the Lawn Lake flood. The flood occurred when Lawn Lake Dam, at the head of Roaring River, broke and released the lake's waters. Sweeping down the steep, forest-bordered streambed, some 674 acre-feet of water left a trail of devastation and destruction. As floodwaters churned into Horseshoe

Park they deposited a coarse, bouldery alluvial fan across the Old Fall River Road at the valley margin, and a veneer of sand, gravel, and silt across much of the valley floor. Six miles downstream the flood spread several feet of fine sand and silt through downtown Estes Park. Above and beyond Horseshoe Park rise the slopes of the Mummy Range, northernmost part of the Front Range. The deep, sheer-walled glacial cirque visible on Mt. Ypsilon's flank contains two glacial lakes, the Spectacle Lakes, not visible from here.

8.5   Many Parks Curve   35.1

Horseshoe Park to the north, Estes Park to the east, and Beaver Meadows and Moraine Park to the south give this viewpoint its name. During the Ice Ages both Horseshoe Park and Moraine Park contained glaciers. Both valleys are edged by straight-topped, thickly forested lateral moraines. Three glacial advances are recognized here, with moraines distinguished by their degree of weathering: The oldest moraines, deeply weathered, are covered with well established soil. The next oldest are less deeply weathered and bear thinner, rocky soil. The youngest, surfaced with sandy soil, are dotted with almost unweathered boulders.

After the retreat of the glaciers, Horseshoe Park contained a shallow lake held behind the terminal moraines. Now almost completely filled in, the lake left the valley floor virtually level and in part marshy. Fall River twists in looping meanders as it seeks a downhill path across the valley. In places it leaves **oxbow lakes** as it shortcuts from one meander loop to another.

From this viewpoint you can also see the many bare granite knobs that surround Estes Park. Unlike metamorphic rocks — mostly schist — that appear farther west, granite tends to weather into rounded shapes.

9.9   Iron Dike (see geologic map)   33.7

Watch the roadcut carefully for this broad, dark gray dike, 50 feet thick, composed of very hard, tough, almost black intrusive rock called **gabbro.** The name Iron Dike is a hand-me-down from mining days, and reflects the dike's high iron content — mostly in the form of the mineral magnetite. The near-vertical dike can be traced from Mt. Chapin in the Mummy Range southeast past Longs Peak to Magnolia, west of Boulder, a total distance of about 40 miles. The dike formed as iron-rich magma from a source below the earth's crust penetrated a deep vertical fissure, probably late in Cretaceous time when the present Rocky Mountains were beginning to rise.

12.1	2 miles above sea level	31.5

12.7	**Rainbow Curve**	**30.9**

From this viewpoint look southeast and just to the left of a vertical swath cleared for skiing. The line of the Iron Dike appears farther to the left as a dim band in which round-topped pines predominate over spire-topped spruce and Douglas fir. The chemical makeup and soil-forming characteristics of the gabbro dike control the types of vegetation able to grow on it.

The colorful rocks that give this viewpoint its name are all granite, weathered in various shades of purple, brown, and orange. Notice the sets of joints that cut through them, and the way that weathering has intensified along the joints.

13.3-13.6	View of small cirque	30.0-30.3

The little cirque visible west of the highway is, with its semicircular shape, precipitous headwall, and rocky moraine lip, a "textbook" example of this type of glacial feature. Formed by a very small glacier, it nevertheless shows features common to almost all cirques. Even in summer it holds a pocket of snow in the position of the former glacier.

14.3	**Treeline**	**29.3**

The upper limit of tree growth is at about 11,000 feet elevation — higher on south-facing slopes, lower on colder north-facing slopes. Close to this limit, trees are stunted and dwarfed. Blasted by fierce and almost incessant high-altitude winds, they hug the ground, growing to leeward in the shelter of their own earlier growth, forming small "tree islands" in the tundra. These islands and the low-growing tundra plants around them help to hold down the meager soil and to prevent rapid runoff of rain or snowmelt.

Above treeline the climate is decidedly arctic — the equivalent of sea-level climates north of the Arctic Circle, some 2000 miles to the north. Trail Ridge Road is bordered with broad sweeps of alpine tundra and, in places, **felsenmeers,** "seas of rock," where jagged rocks are heaved upward by repeated freezing and thawing. Here and there are patches of coarse sand or gravel left as finer material blows away in the wind. Wind and frost are the two most active forces wearing away these uplands now.

Above treeline Trail Ridge Road is bordered with broad sweeps of alpine tundra and felsenmeers of frost-heaved rocks. National Park Service photo.

Scott W. Starratt
Dept. of Paleontology
U. C. Berkeley
Berkeley, Ca. 94720

Lichens grow on the bare rock here, plant-world pioneers able to obtain nutrients from the rock itself. In turn they chemically break the rocks down into a rudimentary soil in which other plants can become established.

15.3 View of Longs Peak 28.3

The flat top of this peak provides a geologic conundrum. It seems to be a remnant of a once widespread erosion surface only fairly recently (on a geologic time scale) lifted to its present position. But what the age of the surface is we can only guess. Is it a remnant of the essentially horizontal surface formed at the end of Precambrian time, some 600 million years ago? Or of a younger surface that resulted from the wearing down of the Ancestral Rockies in Mesozoic time? Or of a still younger surface formed early in Tertiary time? We may never know the answer.

15.7 **Forest Canyon Overlook** 27.9

The Tertiary erosion surface referred to above is now preserved on the flat or gently sloping tops of Terra Tomah Mountain directly across from the overlook, Stones Peak farther to the left, and the Continental Divide country to the right. This surface, formed after initial uplift of the Rocky Mountains 65 to 50 million years ago, was partly destroyed following the later regional uplift that elevated the Colorado Rockies by some 6,000 additional feet. Uplift revitalizes forces of erosion, and this great doming enabled streams and glaciers to carve deeply into the land, shaping the mountains anew.

Deep, glacier-gouged Forest Canyon is almost perfectly straight. Its glaciers eliminated ridges and spurs left by the stream that initially cut a canyon here. The canyon follows a major fault, which also contributes to its straightness. In places the forested canyon floor is edged with lateral moraines that here and there dam small, elongate lakes.

Tributary canyons, also glacier-carved, hold more lakes — alpine tarns in depressions scooped from solid rock. Hayden Gorge, directly across from the overlook, is named for Ferdinand Hayden, a pioneer geologist who more than a century ago inaugurated exploration of this region. Cirques at the heads of Hayden Gorge and other canyons farther west hold light-colored piles of rocky rubble — moraines of the most recent glaciers, small ones formed just a few thousand years ago.

The overlook itself is on a granite knob surrounded by tundra and felsenmeers.

17.1-17.3   Continental Divide view   26.3-26.5

Mountains along the southwestern skyline lie along the Continental Divide. Streams draining their eastern flank flow ultimately into the Mississippi River and the Atlantic Ocean. Those draining their western slopes are tributaries of the Colorado River, with drainage to the Pacific.

Beyond the Divide is the Never Summer Range. Its colorful peaks also mark the Continental Divide. The drainage there is the opposite of that described above: East slopes drain west and west slopes drain east! The Colorado River makes a deep indentation in the Continental Divide, draining both the west slope of the Front Range and the east slope of the Never Summers.

The view from Trail Ridge to Hayden Gorge encompasses many features of glacial erosion: cirques, a troughlike valley, a matterhorn (Hayden Spire), and the Continental Divide arête.

Even late in the summer there may be a snowfield here. Westerly winter winds whipping across Rocky Mountain uplands clean off those uplands and deposit snow in cornices and overhangs on the lee sides of mountain ridges. As a result, snow lies deeper and lasts longer in the lee of the ridges.

Examine the snow closely. Unless there has been a very recent snowfall you will find that it consists of small icy beads. The beads form as ice molecules of snowflakes gradually regroup into more compact spherical form. They are the first step in the formation of glacial ice. With increased pressure from more and more snow, such icy beads fuse into solid ice.

Trail Ridge Road draws its name from an old Ute Indian trail, shown here near the summit of the ridge. Tundra is fragile, delicate, and easily damaged; it takes many years to reestablish itself.

Southwest of the Rock Cut parking area, along the Continental Divide, are several snowfields similar to that described above. If winter snow should consistently exceed summer melting, such snowfields would grow in size and thickness and become icefields. When and if such icefields reached depths of 100 feet or so, the ice would begin to flow downhill, propelled by its own weight and the ever-present tug of gravity. Thus glaciers are made. There are at present three small glaciers, indistinguishable from snowfields at this distance, nestled under the Contintental Divide: one under Mt. Ida directly across from you, one at the head of Hayden Gorge farther east, and one still farther east below Sprague Mountain.

The larger glaciers that once occupied these gorges left behind many signs of their passing: cirques, alpine lakes, grooved and striated rock surfaces, the troughlike gorges themselves, and both lateral and terminal moraines.

A striking feature of the nearer landscape is the contrast between precipitous cliffs and smooth or gently undulating uplands. It is this contrast that led geologists to recognize the two-stage uplift of the present Rockies. Arched and faulted upward late in Cretaceous time, 65 to 50 million years ago, and worn into rounded hills and valleys during the ensuing 20 to 25 million years, the Rockies were then elevated again by broad regional uplift 28 to 10 million years ago. This second uplift rejuvenated streams and rivers and brought about development of mountain glaciers. Water and ice then carved deep cliff-edged valleys, leaving the rounded hills — now the tops of many mountains — more or less intact.

The smooth uplands, particularly those that slope fairly steeply, continue to change. Wet by snowmelt and rain, alternately frozen and thawed, soils creep slowly downslope. In places small mudflows break through the tundra; elsewhere the tundra moves as a mat, a little at a time, creating small stepped terraces. Tongues of loose rock move down across the vegetated slopes.

Alpine flowers grow here in profusion, all hugging the ground, all living out the short growing and blooming season of the tundra. A short walk on the Tundra Trail will give you a close look at some **patterned ground,** where broken rocks

Above timberline, alternate freezing and thawing may rearrange rock fragments into the polygons of patterned ground. National Park Service photo.

lifted and moved about by repeated freezing and thawing form irregular polygons around patches of tundra. Some of the rocks are tilted up as tombstone rocks. The trail also passes a mushroom rock, with a light-colored stem of decomposing granite and a cap of darker, more resistant schist. Which of these rock types is exposed in the Rock Cut along the highway? Notice the twisted, distorted banding of the schist and the light-colored veins of quartz that cut through it.

More patterned ground appears west of the parking lot. On slopes along the Continental Divide is another version of patterned ground — vertical streams of rock and tundra.

19.3 Tundra Curves 24.3

Tundra soils are thin, as roadcuts show. They are also slow to form. In the more than fifty years since the building of Trail Ridge Road, few tundra plants have moved onto exposed roadcut surfaces.

Volcanic rocks of Lava Cliffs may have come from a volcano in the northern Never Summer Range. Iceberg Lake, which once occupied the cirque below these cliffs, drained as its ice dam melted. National Park Service photo.

19.8   **Lava Cliff Cirque**   **23.8**

This viewpoint once overlooked a small cirque lake, nestled close under the cliff. Apparently the lake was dammed by nearly permanent ice in the moraine at the lip of the cirque. Sometime after 1960, however, this ice melted and the lake drained. Now it contains water and icebergs only during summers which follow particularly heavy winter snowfall.

The "lava" cliff is composed of **welded tuff,** a rock that forms when volcanic ash is hot enough to weld itself together as it comes to earth. Notice that it shows some suggestion of vertical columns, formed as vertical cracks developed during cooling. The volcano responsible for this tuff erupted about 28 million years ago, probably in the Never Summer Range.

20.4   More patterned ground   **23.2**

20.6   Highest point on Trail Ridge Road   **23.0**

From this viewpoint the Gore Range, also cored with Precambrian igneous and metamorphic rock, can be seen far to the south. To the west, closer at hand, is the Never Summer Range. It is composed at its southern and northern ends of dark gray Precambrian rocks, but its center is made up of brightly colored Tertiary intrusive rocks.

For eastbound travelers, this overlook offers the first view of Longs Peak to the southeast, identified by its squared-off summit (see eastbound mile 28.3). For westbound travelers the smooth volcanic slopes of Specimen Mountain are now in sight to the west (see mile 22.2, below).

Notice again the abrupt change between flat or gently sloping mountaintops and steep glacier-carved canyon walls.

21.8   Fall River Pass, Alpine Visitor Center   21.8

This visitor center includes displays on geology and tundra processes, but the best exhibits are outside: nearby patches of corn snow, the huge three-lobed cirque at the head of the Fall River drainage, the troughlike canyon of Fall River with its veined and banded walls, the erosion of schist into pinnacled

Snow blown over the crest of the divide accumulates in cornices that may last through the summer. Where and when more snow accumulates in winter than melts in summer, glaciers are born.

ridges on the slopes of Mt. Chapin in the Mummy Range to the northeast, differential weathering of hard granite knobs, patterned ground, and evidence of soil creep.

The trail to the granite knob north of the pass is well worthwhile, and opens up a larger view of the Mummy Range and of Fall River Canyon, with the Old Fall River Road winding up it. Look for examples of soil flow, where wet soils have flowed downhill to form grassy terraces. What other geologic features can you see? Look for patterned ground, felsenmeers, tombstone rocks, avalanche paths, hanging valleys, and glacial tarns.

22.2   **Medicine Bow Curve**   **21.4**

Specimen Mountain, whose pinkish-gray triple summit is now in view to the west, is composed entirely of Tertiary volcanic material — tuff, breccia, and the decomposing remains of some lava flows. The mountain, however, is not the volcano itself, nor is its so-called "crater" a real crater. Most of its volcanic rocks are products of violent explosive eruptions. Between this viewpoint and Specimen Mountain is the straight, glaciated valley of the Cache la Poudre River.

Almost directly north of here are the Medicine Bow Mountains. Beyond them, hazy and indistinct, the white quartzite summits of the Snowy Range lend a snow-capped aspect even in summer. The quartzite is the oldest rock in the area, more than 2.3 billion years old. To the northeast, in the Mummy Range, a well defined glacial cirque marks the side of Comanche Peak, northernmost peak in Rocky Mountain Park. The high crest of the Never Summer Range shows to the southwest across Milner Pass.

The roadcut here exposes Precambrian schist with two pods of light-colored granite.

24.0   Treeline (see westbound mile 14.3)   19.6

25.3-25.6   Volcanic tuff in roadcuts   18.0-18.3

Loosely put together and therefore one of the least stable of rocks, volcanic tuff readily fragments and frequently is the substance of large rockslides such as are seen here.

Poudre Lake is somewhat of an anachronism: a lake right at the summit of a divide. During the last Ice Age a branching arm of the Kawuneeche Valley glacier flowed from west to east across Milner Pass, rounding and smoothing it and shaping the lake's basin.

The Continental Divide runs across the low ridge at the west end of Poudre Lake. Waters of the lake drain northeast via the Cache la Poudre River and the South Platte to the Missouri and then to the Mississippi. On the other side of the divide, drainage is via Phantom Creek to the Colorado River, which before development of dams and water diversion projects emptied into the Gulf of California.

Why is the Continental Divide so much lower than Fall River Pass or the highest parts of Trail Ridge Road? The divide follows an up-and-down line of mountain crests and intermountain passes. Normally, highways wind up stream valleys to the passes — the low points along divides. Because it was built with scenic interests in mind, Trail Ridge Road climbs up a long, high ridge that projects eastward from the divide. Only here at Milner Pass does this highway, having dropped down from Trail Ridge, reach the level of one of the passes.

Unlike many Colorado divides, this one is not knife-sharp.

Pinnacles near Poudre Lake are remnants of a once extensive sheet of volcanic ash. The lake lies almost on the Continental Divide. National Park Service photo.

Instead it is so broad as to have a lake almost on the pass itself. Why? The large rock knob west of the lake offers a clue. Its western side is rounded, its eastern steep and craggy. These features are due to glacial grinding and plucking, and the difference in its two sides indicates that the glacier that shaped it moved from west to east across this pass; the valley west of the pass — Kawuneeche Valley — must at one time have been filled with ice to this level!

Pinnacles across the lake are composed of pinkish tuff and **volcanic breccia.** Composed of angular fragments of volcanic rock embedded in tuff, volcanic breccia is a product of explosive volcanic eruptions such as that which rocked Mt. St. Helens in 1980. Although there is no known volcano in the park, the source of these rocks may be one of several volcanic plugs — solidified volcanic conduits — in the northern Never Summer Range.

26.8 **Lake Irene** **16.8**

This pretty little lake is dammed at its west end by a landslide of volcanic rock, mostly tuff, from Specimen Mountain.

Pretty little Lake Irene, near Milner Pass, is dammed by a landslide from Specimen Mountain.

| 28.2-28.4 | Gneiss in roadcuts | 15.2-15.4 |

There are good exposures of gneiss here, in both roadcuts and natural outcrops.

Along this stretch of highway you may notice the downhill bend of many tree trunks, indicative of deep winter snow and soil creep. Both snow and soil creep tilt young, shallow-rooted trees, which later curve to grow upward again. Older trees with deeper root systems can withstand the soil creep and may even help to prevent it.

| **28.7** | **Farview Curve** | **14.9** |

Kawuneeche Valley, the valley of the upper Colorado River, was shaped by a succession of great glaciers. Glaciers tend to straighten the stream courses down which they flow, and this valley is no exception. Rock crushed and broken by faulting edges both sides of the valley, though, showing that it was a fault valley to begin with and probably fairly straight even before additional shaping by moving ice.

Meadowed bottomlands that partly fill in the valley are bordered by dense forests of ponderosa and lodgepole pines, aspen, and Douglas fir growing on old lateral moraines. Thanks to long-ago damming by terminal moraines, the gradient of the valley is so gentle that the Colorado River winds in sinuous meanders along its floor. In places, meander loops have

The glacier that carved Kawuneeche Valley cut through relatively soft rocks of the Never Summer Range. The valley is wider than most glacial thoroughfares in Rocky Mountain Park, probably because it is downdropped between two faults. National Park Service photo.

been isolated as **oxbow lakes.** Elsewhere beavers, active little geologic agents, have dammed the river or its tributaries. Beaver dams retard erosion and, by collecting silt and organic debris, speed the development of meadows.

The Never Summer Range is composed at both its northern and southern ends of ancient metamorphic rocks, darkly banded gneiss and schist like those in the Front Range to the east. The colorful central part of the range contains much younger volcanic and intrusive rocks, all of Tertiary age, about 25 million years old. Although the intrusive rocks are similar in composition to Precambrian granite of the Front Range, they are much more easily weathered and eroded. Weathering brings out the bright colors — the rust colors of oxidized iron. Because the rock is easily broken down, the central peaks tend to be cone-shaped, in contrast to the sharply angular cliffs and ridges in the Front Range and at the southern end of the Never Summer Range. Note the development of broad open cirques in this area, and the absence of high cliffs. Several cirques now contain **rock glaciers**, humpy, slow-moving masses of broken

The central part of the Never Summer Range is made up of colorful Tertiary intrusive and volcanic rocks too soft to stand in high cliffs. Glacial features, like the two large cirques in the photo, are subdued.
National Park Service photo.

rock, lubricated by ice, that creep gradually downslope. They show up well through binoculars.

Long avalanche paths — funnellike treeless areas where avalanches recur frequently — mark the range, too. The nearly horizontal scar running almost the length of the range marks the Grand Ditch, built near the turn of the century to catch and transfer water from the Pacific drainage across La Poudre Pass to the eastern slope. About 30,000 acre feet of water are transferred each year. Grand Ditch is but one of many diversion projects that lessen the flow of the Colorado River.

The Never Summer and Front Ranges converge at the headwaters of the Colorado River at La Poudre Pass. The pass is accessible by the Colorado River-Little Yellowstone trail.

In the roadcut opposite the parking area are several large lumps of coarse-grained white granite intruded into metamorphic rock.

| 29.1-29.2 | Volcanic ash in roadcuts | 14.4-14.5 |

Light-colored tuff and some dark red-brown lava appear in several roadcuts here. There is gneiss also, much distorted through eons of deep burial and mountain-building.

The Red Mountain and Colorado River-Little Yellowstone trails (discussed in Chapter IV) leave from here.

35.1   Never Summer Ranch   8.5

A pleasant half-mile walk across fragrant clover-filled meadows leads to the Never Summer Ranch, operated during the 1920s as an unpretentious dude ranch. It now serves as a living museum, with jean-and-calico-clad interpreters performing ranch tasks.

This part of the Colorado River was once called the Grand River; the name Colorado was used only below its confluence with the Green River in Utah. Its name was changed by act of Congress in 1921 so that the river would bear the same name as the state in which its headwaters lie.

Walking back to your car you will have the Front Range before you, thickly clothed, as is the Never Summer Range, in a conifer forest. Higher parts of both ranges, above treeline, are not visible from the valley floor. Although the Front Range is composed almost entirely of Precambrian crystalline rocks, here where it converges with the Never Summer Range it does contain some volcanic rock, mostly tuff and welded tuff.

39.0   Onahu Creek   4.6

Dead trees near Onahu Creek were killed as beaver dams flooded the area in which they grew. In the long run beavers undoubtedly increase the supply of trees, for their ponds fill in with sediment and plant material and become meadows capable of supporting new forest. The gradient of the Colorado is very slight here, so the river swings widely in meanders.

40.1-40.3   Gneiss in roadcuts   3.3-3.5

Some of the ancient metamorphic rocks of the Front Range, gneiss and schist about 1.75 billion years old, show up here in roadcuts. Banded in light and dark tones of gray, these ancient rocks resemble those seen in the cores of many mountain ranges and the depths of many canyons in the Rocky Mountain region.

Loose rock material on the other side of the road is part of the lateral moraine of a glacier that came down this valley in Ice Age time.

43.6   **West visitor center**   **0.0**

Moraine Park-Bear Lake Road

Leaving Route U.S. 36 a short distance west of the Beaver Meadows entrance station, this road crosses Beaver Meadows and then zigzags down the lateral moraine that borders Moraine Park on its north side. Unsorted rock debris, from gigantic boulders to fine clay, makes up the moraine, deposited by the great glacier that flowed down the valley of the Big Thompson River.

The Moraine Park Visitor Center is ideally placed for an excellent view of Moraine Park and its glacial features, and of Longs Peak and other glacier-carved summits to the south-west. At the parking lot an engraved sketch of the mountain scene identifies the main features of this view.

Moraine Park is almost surrounded by boulder-studded moraines deposited by the Big Thompson glacier, whose thickness in Moraine Park was probably at least 750 feet — the height of a 75-story building. The north lateral moraine, the terminal moraine downstream, and the long, flat-topped ridge of the south lateral moraine across the valley are all clearly defined topographically. In addition, they are well marked by thick forests, which do well on the water-retentive soil of moraines. The valley is floored with outwash deposits and more recent stream (and possibly lake) deposits. Jutting up through these are a few "islands" of solid rock rounded by glacial action. Upstream beyond the rounded "islands" you can see the glacial trough sculptured by glaciers originating in Forest and Spruce Canyons and Odessa Gorge.

Just beyond the visitor center entry a side road leaves the

Thickly forested, a lateral moraine rises above the nearly level floor of Moraine Park. Background ridges mark the Continental Divide.
National Park Service photo.

Moraine Park-Bear Canyon road, runs past the Moraine Park Campground entrance, and continues west to the upper end of Moraine Park and the Fern Lake trailhead. It stays between the north lateral moraine and the mid-valley rock "islands," and from it you can see that the "islands" are smoothly rounded on their upstream (west) ends and glacially plucked into rough steps on their downstream ends. Such rocks are called **roches moutonnées** (sheep rocks) because of their fancied resemblance to the backs of sheep.

The floor of Moraine Park is almost — but not quite — level: Its center is slightly higher than its margins. Because of this, the Big Thompson River divides and flows along both sides of the valley rather than down its center. A cross-section profile of the valley suggests that it is filled in with glacial outwash, bouldery gravel deposited in front of the receding glacier by meltwater streams.

71

Continuing on the main road toward Bear Lake, the route crosses the terminal moraines that close the lower end of the valley. Near the bridge the Big Thompson River cuts through these moraines, exposing many of the giant boulders brought here by the rivers of ice — boulders much too big to have been carried by the Big Thompson River across the low-gradient floor of Moraine Park. The stream does flow strongly enough to carry away smaller debris, exposing the boulders. Though two or even three terminal moraines can be distinguished in other valleys of the park, it is difficult or impossible to define separate moraines here.

The road crosses the curving end of the terminal moraine, then follows the southern edge of Moraine Park's south lateral moraine, which you can see as the bouldery hill on your right.

From the picnic area at Hollowell Park another unusual feature of this region can be seen. Looking upstream, search for a band of aspen that runs up the hillside slightly to the left of your view. The aspen, light green in summer, yellow in fall, gray in winter, are growing on the Iron Dike, a narrow intrusion of coarse-grained, almost black gabbro. The dike cuts cross-country from Mount Chapin north of Trail Ridge Road to Magnolia, a small town west of Boulder. (See also Trail Ridge Road, in this chapter.) Here the conifers, the evergreens, seem

Mighty boulders once carried by glaciers are now exposed by the Big Thompson River.

to shun the soils derived from the gabbro dike, though the aspen do not seem to mind them. Do you think Hollowell Park is a glaciated valley? Why is its floor so flat?

Leaving Hollowell Park, the road curves eastward around Bierstadt Moraine, then stays on the south slope of that moraine all the way to Bear Lake, with good views of the glacial gorges and high cirques near Longs Peak and the Continental Divide.

At Sprague Lake picnic area several small ponds have been enlarged by increasing the height of hilly natural moraine dams. Flat-topped gravel terraces here, with well rounded pebbles and cobbles, are stream deposits.

As the road climbs higher there are more good views of glacially eroded high country. The striking mountain prow straight up the valley is Hallett Peak, with Tyndall Glacier in the cirque to the right and Flattop Mountain (which doesn't look flat-topped from here) still farther to the right. Otis Peak and Thatchtop Mountain are to the left of Hallett Peak.

At Prospect Canyon, Glacier Creek cuts a deep ravine in much-jointed gneiss. A prospect tunnel follows a narrow and apparently unprofitable vein of quartz. There is no record of sudden wealth from any of the prospect holes and small mines in Rocky Mountain Park. West of Prospect Canyon the highway begins to climb the steep side of Bierstadt Moraine, and on the second switchback reaches the parking area for several of the trails described in Chapter IV. South of the parking lot are Glacier Knobs, steep-sided rock masses that to some degree withstood the might of glaciers coming down Glacier Gorge, Loch Vale, and Tyndall Gorge. Glacially transported boulders on their summits show that the ice at times completely engulfed them, then left these **erratics** as it melted away.

From the Bear Lake parking lot at the end of te road, Hallett Peak dominates the western skyline. To the right of it are the pinnacles and crags of Flattop Mountain. The upper tip of Tyndall Glacier glistens white between Hallett and Flattop.

Thatchtop Mountain, easily recognized by its descriptive name, separates Loch Vale from Glacier Gorge. Its streaky "thatched" summit, part of the rolling Tertiary surface raised by regional uplift, is marked with patterned ground — a surface of tundra and broken rocks rearranged by freezing and thawing of soil moisture. Closer at hand, Glacier Knobs hide most of Glacier Gorge from view. During the Ice Age, glaciers that ground up and over Glacier Knobs probably fragmented into great icefalls. Reforming below the knobs they then flowed on down the valley as far as present-day Sprague Lake and Glacier Basin Campground.

As for the rocks you see from here, most of them are schist or gneiss interlayered with sills of granite. Glacier Knobs, Hallett Peak, and Thatchtop all show the dark bandings of metamorphic rocks and the lighter bands of granite. Longs Peak and part of the high country adjacent to it lack the gneiss-schist bands.

The new alluvial fan at the base of Roaring River sprang into being in a single morning. Some of the boulders in the fan are 20 feet in diameter. Arrow points to large power shovel dwarfed by boulders.

Old Fall River Road

Built between 1913 and 1920, this narrow, now one-way road was the first road across the national park. Today it is marked with numbered guideposts (gp) that correspond with a "motor nature trail" guidebook available where the road begins to climb. The route starts in Horseshoe Park, branching off U.S. 34 about 2.5 miles west of the Fall River Entrance Station.

Where the road crosses the floor of Horseshoe Park there is evidence of the flood that swept down Roaring River early one morning in the summer of 1982. Lake waters broke through a man-made earth dam at Lawn Lake, about 5 miles north of Horseshoe Park, plunged down the Roaring River, and emerged into Horseshoe Park. Within a few hours the Roaring River built a new alluvial fan — a fan that contains boulders as large as 20 feet across. Destroyed by the flood, the Old Fall River Road has now been rebuilt across this fan. Fine rock material — gravel and sand — was swept down the Fall River by the raging waters, which virtually destroyed Aspenglen Campground near the entrance station. Several feet of sand and silt were deposited in low-lying parts of Estes Park and in Lake Estes.

For a better look at flood features along Roaring River itself, hike up the Lawn Lake Trail; it begins at the trailhead a short distance east of the new fan. Features along the trail are described in Chapter IV.

Among the great boulders on the alluvial fan can be found a sampling of rock types from the Mummy Range to the north: pink, red, and gray granite and banded dark gray schist. Some of the granite contains particularly large feldspar and mica crystals.

About a mile beyond the new alluvial fan the road begins to climb through outcrops of pink granite. Views of Horseshoe Park show its long meadow, site of a moraine-dammed lake that is now almost completely filled in with sand, mud, and plant material. The Lawn Lake flood is but one of the many geologic "happenings" contributing to the infilling of this valley, reminding us that geologic processes continue today.

At gp 4, to the right of the road, are several large circular

Lake sediments deposited behind moraine dams flatten the floor of Horseshoe Park. Jack Rathbone photo.

potholes, excavated by rocks whirled in stream eddies and whirlpools. Rounded boulders near the potholes also reflect the work of streams; their large size suggests that both their rounding and the shaping of the potholes were the work of glacier-fed torrents much larger than the present river.

Fall River now occupies a steep-walled chasm cut into the floor of the older glacial trough. Looking back toward Horseshoe Park, you can see the broadly gouged profile that speaks of glacial erosion. In Horseshoe Park itself the floor of the glacial trough is covered by more recent stream and lake deposits.

The road zigzags up the side of the valley, bringing into view the striped face of Mt. Chapin. Metamorphic rocks — gneiss and schist — of the Front Range core are well displayed, alternating with sills of younger granite. The gneiss and schist, 1.75

billion years old, are among the oldest rocks in the park. These rocks recrystallized from older rocks deep below the surface. They are exposed here now only because of uplift and subsequent erosion. Smooth, glacially polished rock surfaces to the right of the road, and the rounded knob in the center of the valley upstream from gp 6, are both expressions of glacial erosion.

The same glacier-rounded knob produced lovely Chasm Falls by forcing Fall River to the north side of the valley. There, swirling in whirlpools over solid rock, the stream cut a series of closely spaced potholes, which have left the channel walls sculptured in a series of rounded curves. Other glacial features border the road west of the falls — glacier-polished and striated rock and a glacial erratic near gp 8. There are also plenty of examples of glacial rounding of the rocky canyon walls.

Watch carefully for the Iron Dike, a broad band of dark, crystalline gabbro that extends from Mt. Chapin to the town of Magnolia east of Boulder. In places the typical trough shape of the glaciated valley is concealed by landslides and rockfalls, which tend to stabilize at about 35-degree slopes. No doubt

Potholes shaped by stream erosion are now high and dry above stream level. Potholes are scoured in a mortar-and-pestle process as streams whirl rocks and gravel in shallow depressions. National Park Service photo.

Many examples of glacial polish and glacial striae can be seen along the Old Fall River Road. National Park Service photo.

many of the slides were initiated at the end of the Ice Ages, when supporting glacial ice melted away, allowing loose ice-carried rocks and solid rock walls to collapse toward the valley floor. Along this part of the canyon, the ice may have been as much as 1500 feet thick.

Examine the canyon walls for avalanche scars and signs of other recent slides, some of them postdating construction of the Old Fall River Road. The large slide across from gp 11 is fairly recent; lichens and other vegetation have not yet developed on the new rock surfaces. Other recent slides, like the one at gp 12, have necessitated rock-and-wire retaining walls to hold the road in place. Above timberline, landslide processes are as important as floods in reshaping the mountain slopes. Many of the slides are also wintertime avalanche chutes, marked by uprooted trees and bent saplings.

Rugged, corrugated ridges on the slopes of Mt. Chapin, directly above the road, result from a whole row of almost parallel landslide and avalanche chutes. Rocks that slide down these chutes accumulate in fan-shaped piles at the bottom of

Avalanche scars are swept clean by winter avalanches and summer rockslides. Loose rocks tend to reshape glaciated valleys. National Park Service photos.

the canyon, and may later be washed away by the stream.

South across Fall River the slopes of Sundance Mountain bear traceries of rock and tundra, patterned ground characteristic of areas where centuries of freezing and thawing of soil moisture break rocks apart and rearrange the fragments into long parallel lines and loops. On gentler slopes rocky polygons may surround undisturbed, almost rock-free patches of tundra. There are many good views of the Sundance Mountain patterned ground as the road continues.

From gp 13 look back down the glaciated valley toward Horseshoe Park and reconstruct in your mind a picture of the great rivers of ice that shaped this valley. In rocky moraines that arch across Horseshoe Park we find evidence of three successive glaciers. In the rounding and grooving of the rock walls we find evidence that at least one of them was more than 1000 feet thick — up to the level at which rounded rock faces give way to angular, blocky, or jagged ones. To become a glacier, an icefield must be about 100 feet thick. At that depth the ice at the bottom becomes plastic and begins to move downhill, carrying the rest along. Successive winters pile on more and more snow, and if the summers do not melt it away the glacier increases in size. Much of the snow for eastern-slope glaciers came from the western slope, blown across the divide by prevailing westerly winds and accumulating as cornices just below the mountain crest. Even today snow cornices at the head of the Fall River valley survive late into the summer.

Above treeline, interlayering of granite and schist across the canyon becomes apparent. Similar rocks on this side are too close for a good over-all view.

There are some excellent examples of glacial striae and glacial polish right beside the road near and above gp 16. Ice itself is not hard enough to cut such grooves, but glacial ice contains rock fragments of all sizes — from huge boulders down to fine glacial flour. Embedded in the ice, the rock fragments are the teeth of the rasp; they grind away at any rocks with which they come in contact. The rock fragments themselves become marked with similar striae, of course, and can often be recognized in moraines.

The same glacier-polished outcrop by the road reveals also the contorted patterns characteristic of some schist. Several large, angular chunks of schist seem to float in lighter granitic rock, as if they were torn from their positions by intrusion of the granite.

The cirques at the head of Fall River Canyon are marked now by soil flow lobes outlined by vegetation. Resulting from freezing and thawing, soil flow has rounded moraine hills in the center of the photo. National Park Service photo.

Once above timberline you'll see that straight, narrow ravines cut down through the glaciated valley floor. They have been cut by stream erosion since the melting of the last glacier some 10,000 years ago.

Across the valley, the vertical white band that stripes the rock wall is a quartz vein. Not many miles to the south, in Colorado's Mineral Belt, such a vein would probably attract prospectors and miners, for gold commonly occurs in quartz veins.

At the head of Fall River's canyon a triple cirque — rather like a cloverleaf in plan — represents the birthplace of the Fall River glacier. Several small stream gorges cut into the floor of the valley here — a floor of **ground moraine,** the last debris dropped by the melting glacier. The little gorges may have been initiated by meltwater from the dying glacier; they are doubtless deepened by runoff from melting snow. Unlike some cirques on this side of the mountain, the triple cirque here does not contain a recent moraine; it apparently did not shelter a glacier of the so-called Little Ice Age 4000 years ago.

Looking across the cirque you can see several lobelike patterns bordered by vegetation. These are soil flow lobes. Unable to drain away through underlying permafrost (permanently frozen ground), water accumulates in the soil until at some point — most often in spring as the snow melts — the soil-water mixture breaks loose and flows downhill.

The high, rolling upland around Fall River Pass is part of the Tertiary erosion surface formed before the last uplift of this region.

Barren rock and untidy rockpiles in upper Tyndall Gorge testify to glaciation as late as 10,000 years ago. Tyndall Glacier lies behind moraines of the Little Ice Age of 4000 years ago. W.T. Lee photo courtesy of USGS.

IV.
Trailside Geology

Bear Lake—Dream Lake—Emerald Lake Trail

Bear Lake is the product of not one glacier but two. At its eastern end it is contained by the terminal moraine of the glacier that carved Tyndall Gorge, north of sharp-prowed Hallett Peak; on the south it is dammed by a lateral moraine of the Chaos Canyon glacier, which flowed from a high cirque between Hallett and Otis Peaks. Both moraines contain large lichen-covered boulders intermixed with gravel, sand, and clay. Rock fragments include both granite and schist.

A nature trail circles the lake, taking you first along the terminal moraine. From guidepost (gp) 9 you can clearly see the nearly horizontal crest of the lateral moraine across the lake.

Just before gp 12 the trail crosses a **talus** slope made up of large angular rock fragments fallen from cliffs above. What rock types do you recognize here? Similar rocks make up the two very large boulders beyond the bench at gp 13. Mineral grains are more or less equidimensional in both these boulders. Do you see any alignment of mineral grains? Can you recognize any of the minerals? The same minerals occur in larger crystals in the coarse-grained pegmatite blocks used to border the trail near gp 14.

Joining the north end of the terminal moraine is another lateral moraine. And ahead, to the west, barren, glacier-plucked rock faces spill talus and rockslide material toward the trail and the lake.

Between gps 22 and 24 the trail is very bumpy and irregular,

One of the many beauty spots of this national park, Bear Lake is dammed by the lateral moraine of the combined Tyndall Gorge-Chaos Canyon glaciers. Longs Peak, background, and rounded Glacier Knobs are brought closer by a telescope lens. National Park Service photo.

for geologic reasons. In places it is breaking and subsiding as plant matter, product of marshy lake margins, compacts or washes away. Elsewhere it is pushed up by the swelling of fine lake clays, or tilted back toward the hill by slow creep of rocks and soil.

At gp 26 the trail climbs onto solid rock and then onto the bouldery lateral moraine that borders Bear Lake on the south. Here, tree roots pry rocks apart along joints; other roots seem determined to hold the rock together. A large boulder at the lake's edge at gp 28 displays the close interrelationship between 1.75 billion year old schist and 1.45 billion year old granite: Fragments of schist are embedded in the granite, and frayed fingers of granite appear to be drawn into blocks of schist.

The lake is filling in now with cobbles, boulders, sand, and tree trunks. In such cold water, decay is slow and wood lasts a long time. Trees that fall within the forest also lie there for many years. Ultimately fallen timber contributes to the build-up of forest soil. A good trail leads on to Nymph, Dream, and Emerald Lakes, higher up on the Tyndall Creek drainage. From the junction of the Bear Lake and Emerald Lake trails there is a fine view of Hallett Peak, with its formidable prow and vertical north face. North of Tyndall Gorge rise the rugged crags that edge Flattop Mountain. The saddle visible between the two summits lies on the Continental Divide.

Boulders along the trail are, again, schist and granite. And again they are mixed with cobbles, gravel, and fine clay or **glacial flour**.

As the trail rounds the rocky knob southwest of Bear Lake, the straight and nearly level crest of a **medial moraine** shows up, marking the line where the Chaos and Tyndall Creek glaciers met the glacier coming down the valley of Icy Brook. Glacier Knobs project above and behind this moraine. In the distance, Longs Peak displays its steep western slope.

The trail curves northward to Nymph Lake, in the cup of a recessional moraine deposited during a still-stand in the retreat of the Tyndall Glacier. On the north side the lake is bordered by granite containing angular fragments of schist, part of the ridge between this and the next drainage. As the trail turns south around this ridge there are again good views of Glacier Knobs and Longs Peak. Jagged pinnacles to the right of Longs Peak have been named the Keyboard of the Winds because strong winds whipping through them sometimes create organ-like sounds audible from the floor of Glacier Gorge. The shoulder of Thatchtop Mountain, farther to the right, displays some patterned ground, alternating streaks of rock and tundra that gave the mountain its name.

The trail steepens as it curves westward. Though the stream is out of sight, it is certainly not out of sound; the tumbling waters are hidden in the forest to your left. Steep granite ledges quarried by glaciers wall the north side of the trail until with several switchbacks it reaches the less precipitous upstream surface of the granite knoll — comparable in shape and position to Glacier Knobs at the mouth of Glacier Gorge.

Dream Lake, long and slender, reflects Hallett Peak's great cliff. Sharpened by repeated frosts, both Hallett Peak and the Flattop pinnacles spill talus toward the valley floor, partly obscuring its typical glaciated form. This lake is dammed by another recessional moraine.

Along the lakeshore the trail is bordered by barren slopes of schist and gneiss, some of them rough with scabs of rock peeling off in thin layers. On many surfaces the scabby layer is all that is left of **glacial polish** — once shiny and smooth as satin.

Watch for striae and large glacial grooves on these exposed rock surfaces.

A short distance beyond the upper end of the lake is an open meadow, an infilled pond. Rocks at the upper end of the meadow run the gamut from schist to granite to coarse-grained pegmatite. Glacial smoothing shows to good advantage the squiggles and wiggles of quartz bands in the schist.

Once moraine-dammed like the lakes below it, Emerald Lake has broken through its barrier so that its present level is determined by the hard bedrock lip of the glacier-scoured basin. Hallett Peak on the southwest and most of Flattop Mountain to the north display bands of schist separated by granite sills. However the northeastern part of Flattop Mountain is almost entirely granite. There the contact between schist and granite is quite distinct, a sloping fault zone with closely spaced parallel faults separating the two kinds of rock. Along the fault zone the younger granite physically forced its way upward into the older schist.

Banded spires of Flattop Mountain are highly fractured or jointed. Talus slopes below are fed by avalanche chutes between the spired ridges. National Park Service photo.

South of Emerald Lake a lateral moraine connects with the terminal moraine. For a better look at the terminal moraine, work your way along the south side of the lake. From there you can also see the steep headwall of the lake basin — not a cirque, because the cirque is higher up, but an exceptionally resistant rock wall that never succumbed completely to glaciation. When a glacier occupied this valley, huge broken fragments of ice must have tumbled in an icefall here.

Energetic explorers may want to undertake the tough scramble up this rock wall and across bouldery glacial rubble to the last tiny alpine tarn, informally called Pool of Jade. Above it are the highest and youngest recessional moraines and the shrunken remnant of modern Tyndall Glacier. Like other modern glaciers in the park, this one came into being about 4000 years ago. It has been shrinking for the past 50 to 100 years.

Glacier Gorge Trail

With an elevation gain of only 700 feet to Mills Lake, the first part of this trail is easy and pleasant. It climbs gradually, rounding the east end of Glacier Knobs. There is a lot of glacial material strewn around — boulders, gravel, and whitish clay — and many bare-rock surfaces smoothed by the glaciers. Glacial polish, striae, and grooves appear on some rock surfaces. These features show up particularly well near Alberta Falls, where there are also a few high-and-dry relict potholes shaped by stream action.

In Ice Age time glaciers flowing from Glacier Gorge and Loch Vale met just above Glacier Knobs and then ground up over them, opening great crevasses as they did so. In all likelihood the scene here then was very much like the scenes of glaciers on Mt. Everest or Mt. McKinley, where icefalls add difficulty and danger for mountaineers. Below Glacier Knobs the rivers of ice reformed to flow on down to the present site of Glacier Basin Campground.

Rock debris here, as well as the bare bedrock itself, is composed of both granite and schist, some of it tinted a rusty red by oxidation of iron minerals. Both rock types show up also on the striped east face of Glacier Knobs, where darker bands are

Tree roots growing in cracks and joints break rocks apart, thereby contributing to soil formation.

marked with contorted, wavy patterns rich in biotite crystals. Some rock faces are streaked with black lichens growing along past or present seepage lines. In fragments of granite, long, parallel feldspar laths show that the thick, partly cooled magma continued to flow as some minerals crystallized out.

As the trail rounds the southern side of Glacier Knobs you will see more and more schist, dark with abundant amphibole and biotite crystals. Glacier Creek cascades among boulders of it. Right at the curve of the trail look for more glacial striae.

Where the trail straightens on the south side of Glacier Knobs, look to the left up Glacier Gorge. The west face of Longs Peak and the jagged ridge of Keyboard of the Winds rise steeply above the gorge. To the left are the ridged cliffs of Half Mountain. Keyboard of the Winds is named for the weird, organlike music that sometimes, when the wind is just right, emanates from its rocky crags. Perhaps you will have a chance to hear its eerie song.

At the trail junction, bear left. (For the **Loch Vale-Sky Pond Trail** bear right and skip to the next section of this chapter.) The trail descends to Icy Brook, then climbs a little. Glacier Gorge is a hanging valley, left far above Icy Brook because the glacier that carved it was not able to cut down as fast as the one that carved Loch Vale. Glacier Creek must tumble in a series of noisy cascades to reach its tributary, Icy Brook, coming from Loch Vale.

There is more glacial polish on rounded rock outcrops near Mills Lake. Ice-dropped boulders are scattered on bedrock surfaces. Notice the upstream rounding and downstream plucking of rock masses, too. The rocks are granite, schist, and in some places dark diorite spotted with whitish quartz crystals. In places, fragments of the 1.75 billion year old schist are enclosed within the 1.45 billion year old granite; elsewhere, granite and schist are interlayered.

Some of the best examples of the rock relationships in the park can be found just before Mills Lake, where the trail crosses a glacially rounded, polished, and striated rock surface. A yard-wide diorite dike crosses the granite-schist outcrop as a dark gray band. Is it older or younger than the surrounding rock?

Mills Lake lies in a basin scooped out by glacial ice. The solid rock dam and several rounded islets in the lake bear adequate testimony to glacial erosion.

Jewel Lake, at almost the same level as Mills Lake, also occupies a glacial basin. Both lakes have sandy deltas at their

Scattered boulders atop Glacier Knobs are glacial erratics dropped as the ice melted.

heads; both are gradually filling in with sand and vegetation. A marsh crossed by the log-walk above Jewel Lake was once a pond.

Above Jewel Lake the trail narrows and steepens, although it remains quite easy to follow. Bare tree roots and an abundance of toppled trees testify to thin, shallow soil. Moss, worn away along the trail, carpets many rock surfaces.

Far to the left, at the top of a steep sliderock slope, the Longs Peak Trail comes through the "Keyhole" to this side of the mountain. The mountain wall approximately parallels expansion joints in the Longs Peak granite — pressure-release joints that formed as the granite, long imprisoned by immense pressures far below the surface, was raised and gradually bared by erosion. The surface continues to wear away: Water seeps into the joints and freezes, exerting pressures sufficient to loosen rock slabs, which then slide down the numerous avalanche and rockslide chutes to the talus piles below.

The Glacier Gorge Trail steepens to surmount a massive, glacially-rounded cliff that holds Black Lake, dark with its own depth. Above the lake, more rounded cliffs head the valley. The lake is dammed by bedrock covered with moraine and rockslide material. In spring and early summer waterfalls splash down the cliffs from the hanging valleys above, where ice once broke into fragments that reformed below in Black Lake's deep basin.

Notice in particular the joints cutting across the granite wall above the lake. Some are pressure-release joints, roughly parallel to the surface. In this rock, vertical joints are few and far between. But granite crags high up to the west are broken by so many vertical joints that freeze-thaw weathering there produced jagged rather than rounded surfaces.

Hardy hikers with topographic maps may want to go on to Green, Blue, or Frozen Lake. The trail follows the only practical route, ascending a steep ravine of rocky rubble that marks a fault zone. Above the cliffs, the routes are indicated by cairns and boot tracks.

The three little lakes, each surrounded by barren slopes dotted with ice-dropped boulders, are backed by the massive cliffs of Longs Peak (14,255 feet), Pagoda Mountain (13,487 feet), Chiefs Head Peak (13,572 feet), and The Spearhead (12,575 feet). A nearly horizontal band of schist stripes Longs Peak, separating the lower steeply sloping surface from the sheer-cliffed summit, where joints are vertical. Similar bands separate sills of light-colored granite on Pagoda Mountain and Chiefs Head Peak. Above Green Lake and Frozen Lake, icefields await a changing climate that might spur their growth into proper glaciers or melt them away altogether.

Looking back down Glacier Gorge you'll see the Mummy Range forming a backdrop for the glacial defile and its string of paternoster lakes, strung out like beads on a rosary.

Near its base, as seen from Green Lake, Chiefs Head Peak bears a sloping band of broken rock (partly hidden by the icefield at the base of the cliff) marking a fault. Without a doubt many faults go unrecognized in these mountains, largely because of the difficulty in discerning displacement when rocks on both sides of faults are identical.

As you start down from these lakes watch the upstream or windward sides of large glacial boulders for the peculiar cup-sized pitting brought about by sandblasting during windstorms.

The U-shaped Ice Age valley gouged by Mills Glacier marks the east approach to Longs Peak. The horseshoe-shaped terminal moraine pushes out into Tahosa Valley. National Park Service photo.

Ice Age glaciers scooped the cirque and "vale" of Loch Vale. The Loch is one of the three lakes in this valley. Taylor Glacier at the head of the valley came into existence about 4000 years ago. Jack Rathbone photo.

Loch Vale — Sky Pond Trail

Branching from the Glacier Gorge Trail southwest of Glacier Knobs, the Loch Vale route proceeds southwest. From the trail junction look south into Glacier Gorge. The steep west face of Longs Peak, as well as the ridged cliffs of Half Mountain, rise steeply above the gorge. Glacier Gorge is a hanging valley: Its stream cascades steeply, at Glacier Falls (hidden among the trees), into the deeper valley cut by the Loch Vale glacier.

The trail to Loch Vale follows the almost straight course of Icy Brook. As you continue up the gorge, compare the rocks on the two sides of the stream. Are they the same, or is there a fault here? The straight course of the stream suggests a fault, though glaciers can be pretty good at straightening out the stream courses down which they flow.

The narrow, V-shaped canyon is clearly not the work of glaciers. It was carved by the stream into the floor of the former glacial trough.

The Loch, which gives its name to the upper valley of Icy Brook, is dammed with solid rock sculptured by the glaciers. Here the valley is glacier-gouged. At its far upper end the slender thread of Timberline Falls plunges over a bare rock barrier. There are two more lakes above the Loch: Glass Lake and Sky Pond. Such lakes, strung out like the beads on a rosary, have been given the name **paternoster lakes**. If you are in shape and have time, continue on to them. Except near the waterfall, where a few ledges must be climbed, it is an easy walk.

Granite and schist, well exposed above treeline, display glacial striae and grooves, and you will see numerous erratics, boulders dropped by melting ice. Some of them are etched by wind.

Fern Lake—Odessa Lake Trail

From the trailhead west of Moraine Park, this route climbs slowly through the glacially carved valley of the Big Thompson River. Boulders of granite along the trail have been carried here by ice, water, and gravity. Though it is not always clear which of these agents is the "prime mover," we do have some basic clues:

• Most glacier-carried rocks are angular; their flat, abraded surfaces may bear striations. Large and small boulders are indiscriminately mixed with coarse and fine gravel and clay, with no apparent sorting, and deposited as distinctive landforms: moraines. Since the rocks may have been moved great distances, rock types are likely to be different from those of their immediate surroundings.

• Stream-borne rocks are nearly always well rounded, even fairly close to their source. Where they occur with sand, silt, and clay they are sorted by size and at least crudely stratified or layered. As with glacial boulders, they reflect upstream rock types.

• Gravity-borne rocks — those that simply fall from canyon walls — are sharply angular and usually lie in piles of talus at the foot of cliffs from which they fall. Though rockfall debris is commonly of the same rock type as that of the cliffs above, talus in glaciated areas such as Rocky Mountain Park may include glacial debris as well.

About half a mile from the trailhead are many loose, angular blocks of rock fallen from cliffs above. The rocks are covered with slow-growing lichens, telling us that these talus slopes probably stabilized some time ago. Much of the rock-falling occurred as the last glacier retreated, when the ice mass that had both sculptured and supported the cliff melted away.

Stop to examine the pink granite that is so common here. Search for a fresh surface, one not covered with lichens, to see

The Big Thompson River tosses in rapids and whirlpools at The Pool, etching out and deepening its channel. National Park Service photo.

the three-dimensional jigsaw puzzle of mineral grains. The pink color of this rock comes from pink feldspar; the colorless, glassy mineral is of course quartz. Black mica, biotite, gives the rock a peppered appearance. There are also crystals of white mica, muscovite.

About a mile from the trailhead some huge boulders known as Arch Rocks lean over the trail. Were they brought here by the stream, by gravity, or by a glacier? They are far too large to have been carried, or even rolled, by the present stream. (It is true that the 1982 Lawn Lake flood carried boulders almost as large, but the canyon down which it came is much steeper than that of the Big Thompson, and peak discharge during the flood far exceeded the Big Thompson's normal flow.) Are these rocks the same as or different from the rock of the cliffs above?

On up the trail, near the bridge over the Big Thompson River, are more giant boulders. How do they differ from Arch Rocks? Take a moment to consider their differences. Boulders of dark gray mica schist are fairly common here; many of them come from the Fern Creek drainage.

Just beyond the bridge take the righthand fork for Fern and Odessa Lakes. The trail climbs across unsorted glacial debris — a mixture of clay, sand, and rocks that makes up the lateral moraine of the Big Thompson glacier. It then leaves this moraine and zigzags up the side of Fern Creek Canyon, almost always within hearing distance of noisy little Fern Creek. Here and there the trees open up enough to allow glimpses of the granite of adjacent slopes, cut with vertical and concentric joints.

Fern Falls are part of a series of cascades down which Fern Creek tumbles some 1200 feet from Fern Lake to the Big Thompson River. Though the dense forest makes it hard to see, the upper valley of Fern Creek is a **hanging valley,** with its mouth high above the Big Thompson River, to which it is tributary. Small glaciers that occupied the hanging valley were never able to cut down as rapidly as the larger ones that flowed down the canyon of the Big Thompson River.

Continuing up the trail you'll see more and more schist and correspondingly less granite among the exposed rocks. Some of the schist is evenly banded in white and dark gray; some is curiously contorted and gnarled, so that it looks like old, weathered wood.

Fern Lake is dammed with a recessional moraine deposited

As seen from Odessa Gorge, Notchtop Mountain displays a glaciated face harboring small icefields. The rock glacier in the foreground moves slowly downstream as water between the rocks freezes and thaws repeatedly. National Park Service photo.

when the retreating glacier stabilized for a time, melting at its tip and depositing its rocky load at this point. The dark emerald waters are backed by forest and, above the trees, by barren rock ridges. To the right the Little Matterhorn juts skyward, like its famous namesake whittled away on every side by glaciers. Everywhere the hand of glaciation is apparent — in rounded rock surfaces, in sharp peaks and narrow arêtes, in rock knobs smoothed on their upstream sides but steep and ragged on their downstream sides, and in the rocky basin occupied by the lake.

The trail crosses the creek at Fern Lake's outlet and follows the east shore of the lake, traveling for a short distance atop a small lateral moraine. Pink and gray granite and dark schist are intermingled here. Watch carefully for glacial grooves and striae and for more rock knobs shaped as glaciers overrode them.

Odessa Lake is less than a mile beyond Fern Lake. Its smooth waters reflect the high peaks and saddles along the Continental Divide — above-treeline country where, now that the glaciers are gone, frost and wind are the primary agents of erosion. Most of the rock of surrounding cliffs is schist striped with sills of granite. To the right are Little Matterhorn and Notchtop Mountain; to the left is Flattop Mountain. Between them lies a deep horseshoe-shaped cirque, birthplace of a glacier, now occupied by two small icefields. A cascade plunges noisily from Tourmaline Gorge west of Odessa Lake, and south of it Grace Falls flings its spray across giant glacier-carved rock steps. The south end of Odessa Lake is filling in gradually with sand and gravel brought down by the stream; a mini-delta extends farther and farther into the lake's quiet waters.

East Longs Peak Trail

The ranger station east of Longs Peak, where this trail begins, lies right on a fault zone, part of the fault system that delineates Tahosa Valley. It is also but a short distance uphill from the Iron Dike, the massive intrusion of black, crystalline gabbro that cuts northwest across Rocky Mountain Park. As the trail zigzags up Pine Ridge, a bedrock ridge surfaced with glacier-deposited rock debris, you'll see a potpourri of angular boulders embedded with no sign of sorting in a matrix of gravel,

Chasm Lake lies just below the east face of Longs Peak. Nestled in the shadow, the present Mills Glacier is far smaller than the one that deposited Mills Moraine. National Park Service photo.

sand, silt, and whitish glacier-ground clay. Except for remnants of some mineralized quartz veins near the Eugenia Mine trail fork (the mine is in the fault zone), all the rock fragments are pale gray granite.

In the glacial rubble most of the larger rock fragments are covered with lichens, but in places you can find a clean surface on which to identify the three principal granite minerals, quartz, feldspar, and mica. In some of the granite, feldspar crystals are long and oriented parallel to each other, showing that the cooling magma continued to flow even as it crystallized, or that the granite, after cooling, later recrystallized to a more gneisslike texture. There are also fragments of schist here, with waving or contorted black and white banding.

Look up from the rocks now and then to notice the changing nature of the forest. Long-needled pines gradually give way to short-needled Douglas fir, Engelmann spruce, and subalpine fir. The pronounced difference in vegetation of north-facing and south-facing slopes is brought about by differences in sunlight, temperature, and retention of soil moisture.

Several rockslides and talus slopes approach the trail along this stretch, reminders that the lateral moraines of glaciers are unstable landforms. Supported partly by the moving ice that creates them, they commonly collapse when the ice melts.

As the trail curves south across Alpine Brook and then climbs steep switchbacks to treeline, it emerges onto alpine tundra whose sea-level equivalent is several thousand miles farther north, in arctic Canada and Alaska. Here at treeline cold, violent mountain winds force the few remaining trees to hug the ground; scrawny "banner" trees grow branches only on their leeward sides. At this elevation wind is a potent factor in erosion. From every exposed patch of ground it blows away the finer particles — fine sand, silt, and clay — leaving only gravel. In addition it lifts and pushes back exposed edges of the tundra mat, then excavates **blowouts.** It even attacks large boulders, sand-blasting scalloped depressions into their upwind surfaces and in some cases etching the surfaces so that they are quite rough.

Where the trail comes out above treeline the view improves. Directly below is Tahosa Valley, dropped down between two faults. To the east across this valley rise Twin Sisters, the highest knobs of a ridge of granite and dark, tightly folded schist.

At the trail fork, bear left for the best views of Longs Peak and the immense cirque below its east face, as well as for the trail to Chasm Lake. The right branch, a slightly shorter, steeper route, passes through Jims Grove, the last stand of dwarfed and gnarled trees.

Boulders of schist become increasingly common. Looking at trailside examples you'll see swirling patterns formed by bands rich in biotite, amphibole, and other dark minerals, alternating with zones of white or nearly white quartz and feldspar.

Several kinds of granite are present here, too: a pink variety whose color comes from pink and red feldspar; a fine, pale gray variety that contains only a very few dark mineral crystals; and a coarse-grained variety with easy-to-distinguish, chunky, interlocking crystals of clear, glassy quartz, silky white feldspar, and both white mica (muscovite) and black mica (biotite). Some granite glitters with long, thin feldspar laths

Alternating layers of granite and schist mark the south wall of the Chasm. Behind rises the granite face of Longs Peak. W.T. Lee photo courtesy of USGS.

oriented parallel or nearly parallel to one another. Both granite and gneiss are heavily decorated with lichens.

At the trail fork bear left toward Mills Moraine, the high rock-covered ridge now visible to the south and southwest. The trail climbs toward a saddle on the crest of this moraine, one of the lateral moraines formed by the glacier that came from the cirque below the east face of Longs Peak. Views from the saddle are magnificent. Far to the east lie the Great Plains, a seemingly flat surface that actually slopes gently away from the mountains. Between mountains and plains is the Colorado Piedmont — the broad valley of the South Platte River. In clear weather it is possible to pick out the hogbacks of upturned Permian and Cretaceous sedimentary rocks along the base of the Front Range. Twin Sisters, the hump-backed ridge to the east and northeast, rises above the Tertiary pediment, which is forested and deeply cut by streams draining the present mountains.

Northeastward, the 8000- to 10,000-foot Tertiary pediment shows up clearly — a very gently sloping surface that is like a broad stairstep between the higher mountains and the Great Plains to the east. Below is Tahosa Valley, downdropped between two faults. And on the slope up which we have climbed it is not difficult to make out the lateral and terminal moraines of the Ice Age glacier that coursed down this side of Longs Peak.

The flanks of Mt. Meeker, to the south across a deep glacial gorge, are striped dark and light with 1750 million year old gneiss and 1450 million year old granite, in a pattern repeated through much of this national park. Longs Peak, on the other hand, is unstriped — a solid mass of pink granite (now partly covered with gray lichens) that invaded the gneiss about 1450 million years ago.

The east face of Longs Peak, the famous "Diamond," is one of the highest cliffs in the Rockies. It is the headwall of the great cirque that now shelters Chasm Lake and small Mills Glacier, both out of view from this part of the trail. Peacock Pond lies in a glacier-carved basin between the trail fork and the north face of Mt. Meeker.

From Mills Moraine the **Chasm Lake Trail** (see next section) runs southwest along the south slope of Mt. Lady Washington. The trail to Longs Peak angles northwest across the east slope of the same mountain. In the broad valley above Jims Grove, soil flow terraces support a series of small ponds. These terraces develop because of permafrost, permanently frozen ground below soil level. Permafrost seals the ground so that water can't sink in. During thaws the water-saturated, semifluid soil flows across the permafrost like wet cement, creating the stepped terraces.

At Granite Pass the trail meets the North Longs Peak Trail, coming up from Glacier Creek and the Bear Lake area. Here there are splendid views northward to the Mummy Range and northeastward to the granite knobs of Lumpy Ridge beyond Estes Park. Notice the nearly horizontal silhouette of the Tertiary pediment beyond these granite hills. Between here and the Mummy Range are two deep valleys, the Fall River Canyon-Horseshoe Park valley, and the Forest Canyon-Moraine Park valley. They are separated by Trail Ridge, with Trail Ridge Road winding up it. Farther to the west are the Continental Divide peaks and the distant summits of the Never Summer Range.

Rounding the north spur of Mt. Lady Washington, the trail zigzags up to the Boulder Field. And that is a misnomer! Dic-

The north face of Longs Peak supplies most of the rock streams that merge with the Boulder Field. Loose rocks in the foreground are 5 to 20 feet across. National Park Service photo.

tionary definitions emphasize that boulders are large **rounded** rock fragments. This area is more correctly termed a **felsenmeer**, an area covered with angular blocks of rock derived from well-jointed bedrock by frost action.

From the upper part of the Boulder Field, part of the Diamond is again in sight. Except for two or three curving, near-horizontal joints, the exposed face of the peak shows only vertical joints. Glaciers that developed on the east face of the peak repeatedly tore away rock along these joints, eventually quarrying the thousand-foot cliff. The strong constitution of the ancient granite has made Longs Peak the highest (and most-climbed) peak in the park: 14,255 feet in elevation.

The north shoulder of the peak, nearer to the trail, bears many curving, more or less concentric joints of the kind we

Giant rock slabs broken and shifted by frost action lead to the Keyhole on the Longs Peak Trail. W. T. Lee photo courtesy of USGS.

often see in massive intrusive rock that has been exposed at the surface. These pressure-release joints are as important in the origin of the Boulder Field as the widely spaced vertical joints are in the origin of the Diamond. With moisture seeping into the pressure-release joints, and repeatedly freezing and thawing there, rock slabs are little by little lifted and tilted and broken away from their neighbors to create the felsenmeer.

The Keyhole is framed by rocks jointed in a similar manner. Along the Keyhole ridge, joints parallel to either side of the ridge come together to form a knife-edge plate of rock. The Keyhole, where pieces of the rock have fallen away, furnishes a gateway to the more easily climbed west side of the peak.

At the Keyhole quite a few of the granite slabs are highly polished and striated, not with glacial polish and striae as you

With many freeze-and-thaw nights and days, rock slabs are dislodged to skid down the steep west face of Longs Peak into Glacier Gorge. Pyramid Peak rises beyond the Keyboard of the Winds. W.T. Lee photo courtesy of USGS.

might at first suspect, but with slickensides, the shiny, grooved surfaces that form along faults. The slickensides tell us that there was some rock movement as the erstwhile joints developed — enough movement to alter the surfaces. Here, the dividing line between joints and faults is narrow, and some of the joints should correctly be termed faults.

On the west side of Longs Peak, rock slabs break off along sloping pressure-release joints and hurtle downward toward Glacier Gorge, leaving behind the steep, smooth rock face seen from the Keyhole. The view west from the Keyhole shows the line of high peaks and saddles along the Continental Divide. Glacier Gorge, below the Keyhole, heads in a pair of cirques occupied now by Green Lake, Frozen Lake, and several small icefields. Many glacial features can be seen from here — U-shaped valleys, narrow arêtes, matterhorn peaks, cirques, moraines, and strings of little lakes called, because of their resemblance to the beads of a rosary, paternoster lakes.

From here also, several remaining portions of the flat or rolling Tertiary upland can be distinguished. The closest is Thatchtop, beyond Glacier Gorge.

Beyond the Keyhole the trail is marked with red and yellow targets. It traverses the steep west face of Longs Peak and then climbs the so-called Trough, a steep, narrow ravine. At the Narrows you'll have a close look at an arête. A last granite slope leads to the top.

The flat summit is the object of a bit of geologic guesswork. Basing their guess on the Precambrian-Cambrian contact in many Colorado canyons, as well as in Grand Canyon in Arizona and the Grand Tetons of Wyoming, some geologists think that it may be an elevated remnant of the eroded plain that existed at the end of Precambrian time. Others point to the horizontal contact between Precambrian and Pennsylvanian rocks at the north end of the Front Range, and maintain that the mountain's flat top is a lifted-up remnant of that surface. Still others believe it is part of the hilly Tertiary erosion surface seen elsewhere in the park, lifted a good deal higher and cleaned off by such alpine processes as freeze-thaw weathering and wind erosion. Take your pick!

Much of the mountainscape visible from the summit, scraped and scoured and deeply gouged by glaciers, has already been described. The Indian Peaks to the south lie along the Conti-

nental Divide. Be sure to peer down on Chasm Lake 2500 feet
below. I need not warn you not to go too near the edge!

Scott W. Starratt
Dept. of Paleontology
U. C. Berkeley
Berkeley, Ca. 94720

Chasm Lake Trail

The Chasm Lake Trail branches from the East Longs Peak
Trail (see preceding section) at the summit of Mills Moraine.
Along the trail as it traverses the south side of Mt. Lady
Washington is the first trailside bedrock on this entire route:
schist and granite similar to that striping Mt. Meeker. Beyond
these rocks is some gray-green, very fine-grained rock salted
and peppered with large white feldspar crystals and small
black rods of amphibole. Igneous rocks in which large crystals
are embedded in a finer groundmass are referred to as
porphyritic; usually they have cooled more rapidly than other
coarse-grained igneous rock. This rock occurs in a sill, an
intrusion that parallels the layering of granite and schist, and
it is much younger than either, having squeezed in between
their layers in Tertiary time. The sill is exposed low on the side
of Mt. Meeker as well as here along the trail.

Far below the trail, the Roaring Fork flows in a stair-stepped
chasm carved by the same glacier — a river of ice many hundreds of feet thick — that deposited Mills Moraine. The ice
flowed from the large cirque directly below Longs Peak, now
the site of Chasm Lake and tiny Mills Glacier. On the canyon
floor directly below the trail, Peacock Pool lies behind a dam of
glacier-smoothed rock. A smaller lake occupies another step
some distance downstream. The rock wall behind Peacock Pool
displays the same porphyry sill that is at trailside, gray-green
rock weathering to a pale orange. The upstream end of Peacock
Pool is filling in slowly with a delta of fine sediment brought in
by the Roaring Fork as it tumbles down from Columbine Falls.

Watch along the trail for other evidence of glaciation: **glacial polish**, **glacial striae**, and crescent-shaped **chattermarks** that show where rock crunched against rock. Crossing
the rock lip near the head of Columbine Falls, the trail itself
follows a glacier-cut groove. Imagine a slow-moving glacier
here, filling the entire gorge, depositing Mills Moraine along
its edge.

Behind the patrol cabin the official trail ends. Boot marks

The precipitous headwall of Chasm Cirque rises 2400 feet above Chasm Lake. The snowbank part way up is the present Mills glacier. W.T. Lee photo courtesy of USGS.

and rock cairns lead up the last great step into the cirque occupied by Chasm Lake and Mills Glacier. Hidden here in the shadows of Mt. Meeker and Longs Peak, the lake may remain frozen well into the summer. It's easy to see how in Ice Age time enough snow could have collected here to build up a glacier. Rock fragments resting where the melting ice dropped them remind us that it has not been long — less than 4000 years — since a glacier of the Little Ice Age filled the cirque of its larger ancestor.

Behind Chasm Lake rises the dramatic east face of Longs Peak and the notorious "Diamond," a world-class challenge for climbers. Its shape and sheerness are controlled by vertical joints in the granite. At the base of the cliff are talus cones of accumulated angular boulders loosened and pried from the rock face by frost — a process going on today. The sheer cliff was of course initially excavated by the successive glaciers that occupied the cirque. Time and time again glacial ice froze to the mighty wall of granite, then pulled the rock away. The pink granite of Longs Peak appears to be more resistant than the granite layered with schist on adjacent mountains; joints are far apart and there are no dark bands of schist weakened by parallel crystals of mica.

On Mt. Lady Washington to the north and Mt. Meeker to the south, avalanche tracks end in piles of rocky rubble. Vertical streaks on the cliffs are patches of lichen growing along seepage lines where small amounts of water, filtering through joints in the rock, reach the surface.

As you leave this lovely lake and its steep-walled cirque, look on the sides of scattered boulders for clusters of cuplike indentations formed by sand-blasting during severe mountain windstorms.

Lawn Lake Trail

It's easy to forget that geology is not just a story of the past. Geologic processes are going on today. There is no better place to become aware of this than the Lawn Lake Trail, with its evidence of erosion and deposition caused by the 1982 Lawn Lake flood.

Before starting on this hike drive beyond the trailhead to see the alluvial fan below Roaring River. The fan was built early in the morning on July 15, 1982 as huge boulders tumbled like pebbles in floodwaters raging downstream from the broken Lawn Lake Dam. Even in the relatively short distance (less than 6 miles) between the dam and the mouth of the stream, rocks were battered and rounded, trees were bruised and splintered.

The trail starts out steeply, with switchbacks leading up the forested wall of Horseshoe Park. At first, few rocks are to be seen. About a mile up the trail, however, are some good views of the raw new ravine of Roaring River. An impressive sight!

Giant boulders tossed like pebbles in the Lawn Lake flood now lie where Roaring River disgorges into Horseshoe Park.

Some 10,000,000 cubic feet of material removed from this V-shaped furrow are now distributed in the alluvial fan, across the meadows adjacent to the fan, and all the way downstream to Lake Estes. The rock debris was sorted according to size: The coarsest material—large boulders—remained in the fan; somewhat finer gravel spread out on the floor of Horseshoe Park; still finer debris—mostly and and mud—was deposited along the Fall River from Aspenglen Campground to Estes Park, where it piled up two feet deep in the streets of the town. The flood wave reached the town about 3½ hours after the dam broke. Mixed with the finer material were boulders and cobbles swept from moraines at the lower end of Horseshoe Park.

About 1½ miles above the trailhead the trail is at stream level. Rocks and sand carried by the flood are well cleaned off — no lichens and no signs of weathering remain. Cobbles and boulders of granite, schist, and gneiss are tossed like marbles in the streambed; many show little crescent-shaped chattermarks where rock pounded against rock. Broken and splintered tree trunks are common in this lower part of the gorge, but will be less common as you approach treeline.

Near the Ypsilon Lake trail junction, where parts of the trail were washed out, the new trail lies right on flood-deposited sand. Watch the high stream banks for stratified, stream-deposited gravel and unsorted glacial moraine deposits. Where the trail rises above the canyon floor there are increasing numbers of boulders of pink and red granite and dark gray schist, heavily decorated with lichens. Some of the granite contains feldspar crystals several inches long. Veins of pinkish quartz occur here too.

About 4 miles above the trailhead, good exposures of schist can be seen in the streambed as well as above it and along the trail. Coarse bands of darker and lighter rock are intersected by veins of white quartz and feldspar. Shiny pieces of mica schist show up in the trail.

After more switchbacks the trail climbs onto a recessional moraine, which apparently held back the floodwaters for a time. Finally this natural dam gave way. Subsequent flood erosion produced an interesting cross section of the moraine. Dark gray clay near the base of the moraine suggests that a lake existed here for a time after the retreat of the glacier. Above the recessional moraine the trail runs for a short distance along the crest of a lateral moraine.

Mummy Mountain rises north of this part of the trail; beyond the Black Canyon trail junction the Lawn Lake Trail veers left to run along the mountain's base. The great granite mass, deeply cut by vertical joints, also displays concentric pressure-release joints caused by expansion of the rock itself.

In the area just below Lawn Lake the flood waters disgorged into a wide, open valley. The devastation here, with wildly piled boulders and splintered tree trunks scattered like matchsticks, is a measure of the fury of the flood. Here again are rounded rocks of many sizes, some marked with crescent chattermarks, and expanses of new, clean sand. All the flood effects, from Lawn Lake to Lake Estes, resulted from the abrupt release of some 674 acre-feet of water. Peak discharge was 18,000 cubic feet per second.

Lawn Lake is now sightly smaller than it was before construction of the Lawn Lake Dam. Since the flood it has been held in by a natural granite rim; prior to dam building a recessional moraine held the water at a slightly higher level. Built in 1903, the dam saved spring runoff for summer farming needs; when released, the water flowed downstream into the Big Thompson River and distributary irrigation ditches. There are no plans to rebuild the dam.

The trail continues to Little Crystal and Crystal Lakes, glacial paternoster lakes which lie in the great cirque between Mummy Mountain and Fairchild Mountain. Though there is no glacier in this beautiful cirque now, many glacial features, including grooved and striated rocks and ground moraine

Where gradients are low, as on the nearly flat lake deposits that floor Kawuneeche Valley, the Colorado River twists and winds, providing homes for beaver, muskrat, and waterfowl. National Park Service photo.

(scattered, as its name suggests, over ground where a glacier melted), can be seen in the cirque. The side of Fairchild Mountain that faces Lawn Lake is composed of the same pink granite as Mummy Mountain, complete with vertical and pressure-release joints. On the southwest flank of Fairchild, though, slanting bands of dark schist extend down to the schist you saw in the streambed of Roaring River.

Colorado River—Little Yellowstone Trail

This trail begins at the Colorado River trailhead and follows the Colorado River toward its headwaters. In the first mile or so it skirts the edge of the valley floor, then passes among lichen-covered boulders and crags of gneiss, with some development of small rock glaciers, slowly moving masses of broken rock. It soon begins to climb across rocky alluvial fans deposited by tributary streams as they reach the flat valley floor, and across talus piles of fragmented, angular rocks. Occasional glimpses to the west reveal beaver ponds and meadows in the river valley, and beyond them the densely forested lower slopes of the Never Summer Range. Here and there are yellowish outcrops of decomposed volcanic rock.

Nearly 2 miles from trailhead, a talus slope to the right is made up of seemingly newly broken rock fragments, with no soil or lichens. These are the tailings of a mine operated by Joe Shipler back in the 1880s and 90s. The mine entrance is at the top of the tailings, in a vein that cuts northeastward up the hill. Shipler was in all likelihood attracted by the red-brown color of the rock in the vein, often an indication of mineralization.

As you proceed northward, notice how thin the forest soil is. Roots are just below the surface or, where hikers' feet have scraped the trail bare, right at the surface.

Farther along, the trail forks, with the left branch dropping down to Lulu City and the right one continuing on to Little Yellowstone. The Lulu City branch eventually rejoins the Little Yellowstone trail. Lulu City was, for all its remoteness, a well planned little mining community, with a town plat showing a rectangular pattern of "city" streets. In terms of mining activity, though, pickings were slim, and the town was abandoned after only 5 years. Today nothing remains but some fallen cabins.

Continuing toward Little Yellowstone, the main trail crosses Specimen Creek, which cascades off Specimen Mountain to join the Colorado. The trail is mostly in the trees, but does cross several barren slopes of rock chips — slopes that creep downhill so constantly that vegetation cannot gain a foothold. If you look carefully through breaks in the forest barrier you can make out, on the Never Summer slope, some of the small mine dumps above Lulu City.

The Shipler Mine, along the Colorado River trail, is typical of small prospect and mine tunnels in the Front Range. National Park Service photo.

About 4 miles above the trailhead the route crosses the Colorado River, much smaller here than down in the valley meadows. It is also much faster moving, thanks to the steeper gradient. From here on we can call it a creek and not a river.

Some of the creek-bed cobbles are shiny mica schist or salt-and-pepper gray granite — Precambrian rocks. But by far the greater number are volcanic tuff in various shades of greenish and pinkish gray. Most of the volcanic rock is fine-grained and composed of rhyolite deposited as volcanic ash, probably as the result of volcanic explosions similar to the 1980 eruption of Mt. St. Helens in Washington. Some of these rocks are porphyritic, containing large, bright crystals of feldspar embedded in the dull, fine-grained matrix.

Just across the bridges is another outcrop of Precambrian schist, shiny with mica. Watch for the contact between these Precambrian rocks and the much younger volcanic rocks. It is not hard to find, a short distance beyond Lady Creek. Geologists trace and map such contacts as the first step in geologic studies. The volcanic rock is poorly consolidated and densely fractured, so it breaks up readily and forms light gray soil and steep, mobile slopes almost barren of vegetation. Where there are trees, the curves in the bases of their trunks are a sure sign of soil creep.

It is this loose, fragmented, sliding rock and the steep-walled

The steep, sharp pinnacles of Little Yellowstone bring to mind the canyon of the Yellowstone River in Wyoming.

canyon that has been eroded in it that suggested the name "Little Yellowstone." The resemblance to the canyon of the Yellowstone River isn't entirely accidental, for there, too, soft volcanic rocks have eroded into a steep-walled gorge. The famous yellow coloring, due to oxidized iron, is absent here, where volcanism was neither as great nor as long-lasting as in Yellowstone National Park.

As the trail climbs to the west rim of Little Yellowstone canyon, step close to the rim and look down on the narrow, steep-walled defile. A few sharp pinnacles of tuff add a bizarre touch to the scenery. They have not been studied in detail, but they may represent the walls of narrow vertical channelways through which volcanic vapors escaped from the cooling ash. Such vapors are known to cement volcanic ash more tightly, increasing its ability to withstand erosion.

A geologic puzzle presented by this little canyon (as well as by the larger Grand Canyon of the Yellowstone) is how such a narrow, V-shaped canyon can have developed in an area otherwise characterized by broadly gouged glacial valleys. Both upstream and downstream from Little Yellowstone, the valley of the Colorado shows evidence of glacial erosion. Yet the sharp pinnacles of relatively soft rock rising from the floor of the canyon here could not have survived glaciation. The Little Yellowstone canyon must have developed during and after the retreat of the last glacier only some 10,000 years ago. Recalling the V-shaped gorge left by the 1982 Lawn Lake flood in the eastern part of this park, it's easy to understand the damage that can be inflicted by running water, particularly in soft, weak material such as this volcanic ash.

Above Little Yellowstone the trail climbs through forest and meadow to Grand Ditch, and follows the ditch to La Poudre Pass. Built early in this century, this ditch carries west slope water over La Poudre Pass to the eastern slope. Near the pass lie the headwaters of the Colorado River, their flow lessened by diversion of small tributaries into Grand Ditch. There are good outcrops of Precambrian rock along Grand Ditch: massive, streaky gneiss shiny with mica. Other outcrops at the pass have a story to tell: Rocky islands in the summit marshes, several of gneiss and one of light-colored volcanic tuff, are shaped somewhat like inverted teaspoons, characteristic of rocks shaped by moving ice. Their gentle north slopes and steep south slopes tell us that the ice here at the summit moved from north to south across the pass, crossing the Continental Divide from Atlantic to Pacific drainage. Now Grand Ditch carries west-slope water in the opposite direction.

Grand Ditch carries water from Colorado River tributaries in the Never Summer Range. The Little Yellowstone trail follows the ditch to Poudre Pass. National Park Service photo.

Glossary

Alluvial fan: a fan-shaped mass of gravel and sand deposited by a stream as it issues from a narrow mountain valley.

Amphibole: a group of dark, rock-forming minerals common in intrusive igneous rocks.

Anticline: a fold that is convex upward, and that has the oldest rocks near the center.

Arête: a narrow, jagged mountain ridge sculptured by glaciers, commonly due to headward growth of cirques.

Augen gneiss: metamorphic rock containing clustered dark minerals surrounded by white areas depleted of those minerals, so that they look like eyes.

Batholith: a very large mass of igneous rock intruded as molten magma, often formed in part by melting and recrystallization of older rocks.

Biotite: black mica.

Breccia: volcanic rock consisting of broken fragments thrown from a volcano, cemented together with lava or volcanic ash.

Cementation: a process by which sediments such as sand and gravel become lithified, or turned to rock, as minerals are deposited between the original grains.

Chattermark: small curved scars or cracks made by rock fragments carried in the base of a glacier or in a rushing stream.

Cirque: a deep, usually steep-walled, semicircular basin excavated by the head of a glacier.

Cleavage: the tendency of many minerals to break or split along certain planes.

Columnar joints: vertically arranged, polygonal joints due to shrinkage accompanying cooling of lava, ash, or magma in a sill.

Compaction: reduction in bulk volume of sediments due to the weight of overlying rocks.

Conglomerate: rock composed of rounded, waterworn fragments of older rock, commonly in combination with sand.

Crossbedding: oblique or slanting laminae between the main horizontal layers of sedimentary rock.

Crystalline rocks: rock consisting wholly of crystals, especially intrusive igneous rock and metamorphic rock that has undergone recrystallization.

Differential erosion (or weathering): erosion (or weathering) at different rates governed by differences in resistance or hardness of rocks.

Dike: a thin body of igneous rock resulting when magma intrudes and cools in a vertical crack or joint.

Diorite: a dark-colored intrusive rock commonly occurring as dikes and sills.

Era: the largest geologic time unit, measuring in hundreds of millions of years.

Erratic: a large rock fragment carried by glacier ice and deposited far from its original source.

Exfoliation: the process by which concentric plates, scales, or flakes of rock successively break loose from a rock mass.

Extrusive rocks: igneous rocks that cool on or very near the earth's surface; volcanic rocks.

Fault: a break in the rock along which both sides have moved relative to each other.

Fault plane: a fracture surface along which fault movement takes place.

Fault zone: a zone of numerous small fractures along which movement has taken place.

Feldspar: a group of abundant light-colored rock-forming minerals.

Felsenmeer: an alpine surface covered with angular rock fragments broken by freezing and thawing of moisture in rock fractures.

Fold: a curve or bend in rock strata.

Formation: a mappable unit of rock.

Gabbro: a dark gray to black, crystalline igneous rock.

Glacial flour: very finely ground rock material produced by the grinding of rocks imbedded in glacial ice.

Glacial groove: a deep, wide, usually straight furrow cut into bedrock by rocks imbedded in the ice of a glacier.

Glacial polish: a smooth surface produced on rock by glacial scouring.

Glacial striae: long, delicate, parallel furrows inscribed on bedrock and rock fragments by the rasping of rocks brought in contact by the movement of glacial ice.

Glacier: a large, long-lasting mass of ice thick enough to move slowly downslope or outward because of its own weight.

Gneiss: a coarse-grained metamorphic rock with alternating bands of granular crystalline minerals such as quartz and feldspar, and fine dark minerals such as biotite.

Granite: coarse-grained intrusive igneous rock having feldspar and quartz as the principal minerals.

Grus: disintegrated granite weakened by the decomposition of some of its mineral grains.

Hanging valley: a glacial valley whose mouth is high up on the wall of a larger glacial valley.

Hematite: a common iron oxide mineral that lends its red-brown color to many sedimentary rocks as well as to brick, tile, and rust.

Hornblende: a common dark green, black, or brown mineral of the amphibole group.

Igneous rock: rock formed by the cooling of molten magma.

Intrusive rock: igneous rock created as magma cools without reaching the surface.

Joint: a rock fracture along which no significant movement has taken place.

Lateral moraine: a ridge-like mass of broken rock and gravel deposited along the side of a glacier.

Limonite: a yellow-brown iron oxide mineral.

Magma: molten rock.

Magnetite: a black, magnetic, iron-rich mineral.

Matterhorn: a glacier-sharpened peak.

Metamorphic rock: rock derived from pre-existing rock altered by heat, pressure, and other processes.

Metasedimentary rock: sedimentary rock altered by heat, pressure, and other processes but still retaining identifiable sedimentary features such as layering, alternating rock types, or ripplemarks.

Mica: a group of complex minerals characterized by closely spaced parallel layers that can be split apart easily.

Mica schist: silvery, lustrous schist in which mica is the most abundant mineral.

Migmatite: gneiss containing sheets and veins of granite seemingly injected into older metamorphic rocks.

Minerals: naturally occurring inorganic substances with characteristic chemical compositions, the prime constituents of all rocks.

Moraine: rock debris deposited by a glacier.

Mudstone: sedimentary rock composed of clay and silt particles.

Muscovite: white mica.

Normal fault: a fault in which the overhanging upper wall moves downward relative to the lower wall.

Outcrop: rock exposed at the surface.

Outwash: stratified sand and gravel deposited by streams or meltwater draining from a glacier.

Overburden: any rock material overlying other rock material.

Patterned ground: polygons, stripes, and other patterns of broken rock material rearranged by repeated frost action.

Paternoster lakes: a series of small lakes strung out along a glacially eroded valley.

Pediment: a broad, gently sloping surface, floored with bedrock, eroded at the base of a receding mountain front.

Pegmatite: exceptionally coarse-grained igneous rock usually found as dikes or veins near the margins of large igneous intrusions.

Peneplain: a land surface worn down by erosion to a nearly flat plain.

Period: a subdivision of geologic time smaller than an era, measured in tens of millions of years.

Permafrost: permanently frozen ground.

Plug: a pipelike core or lava—filled conduit of an eroded volcano.

Porphyritic: igneous rock that contains conspicuous large crystals (phenocrysts) in a fine-grained matrix.

Pothole: a small circular depression excavated by the grinding action of pebbles, cobbles, and sand swirled by running water.

Pressure-release joint: concentric jointing that occurs in once deeply buried rock released by erosion from its confining pressure. Some pressure-release joints form as glacial ice melts, lessening the burden on rocks below.

Recessional moraine: a glacial moraine formed during a temporary pause in the recession of a glacier.

Reverse fault: a fault in which the overhanging wall moves upward relative to the footwall.

Rhyolite: light gray volcanic rock with large quartz and feldspar crystals in a finer groundmass, the fine-grained volcanic equivalent of granite.

Roches moutonées: glacier-rounded rocks with a gentle upstream slope and a steep or stepped downstream face.

Rock glacier: a mass of angular rock fragments with enough interstitial ice to lubricate slow downhill movement, the entire mass having somewhat the same form as a glacier.

Rotten granite: granite weakened by decomposition of some of its mineral grains, principally mica.

Schist: crystalline metamorphic rock which tends to split along parallel planes (usually parallel mica flakes), commonly formed from fine-grained sedimentary rock.

Sedimentary rock: rock made of fragments of earlier rock, animal shells, or chemicals precipitated from water, usually accumulating in well defined layers.

Sill: a flat igneous intrusion inserted between layers of stratified rock.

Slickenside: a scratched and polished surface resulting from fault movement.

Soil flow: downhill movement of saturated soil.

Stock: a medium sized mass of intrusive igneous rock, smaller than 40 square miles at the surface.

Stratified: layered.

Syncline: a fold that is convex downward and that when eroded has the youngest rocks near the center.

Talus: accumulated rock fragments lying at the base of a cliff from which they have fallen.

Terminal moraine: an arc-shaped pile of rock debris that marks the farthest advance of a glacier.

Thrust fault: a low-angle (nearly horizontal) fault on which older rocks slide over younger ones.

Tuff: a rock composed of compacted volcanic ash.

Tundra: a treeless high-altitude surface overgrown with mosses, lichens, low shrubs, and small flowering plants.

Vein: a thin, sheetlike intrusion, commonly with associated mineral deposits.

Volcanic plug: see plug.

Welded tuff: rock formed of volcanic ash fused by its own heat, the heat of volcanic gases ejected with it, and the weight of overlying ash.